DAVID BECKHAM

headline

First published in 2013 by
HEADLINE PUBLISHING GROUP

3

Cataloguing in Publication Data
is available from the British Library

Hardback ISBN 978 0 7553 6589 0

Design and art direction by Patrick Insole
Picture research by Cathie Arrington

Typeset in Fairfield and Linotype Didot

Printed and bound by L.E.G.O. SpA, Vicenza, Italy

Headline's policy is to use papers that are natural,
renewable and recyclable products and made from
wood grown in sustainable forests. The logging and
manufacturing processes are expected to conform to
the environmental regulations of the country of origin.

HEADLINE PUBLISHING GROUP
An Hachette UK Company
338 Euston Road
London NW1 3BH

www.headline.co.uk
www.hachette.co.uk

ACKNOWLEDGEMENTS

Thanks to Matthew Syed of *The Times* for helping
me get my thoughts and reflections on the page.

I am grateful to Patrick Insole, Jonathan
Taylor and the whole team at Headline for all
their hard work on my book.

To Victoria, Brooklyn,
Romeo, Cruz and Harper.
I could never have lived
my dream without you all
by my side. This is for you all.
Love David (Daddy)
xxxxx

THE MOMENT I KICKED

a ball as a child, I realised it was all I ever wanted to do. I still have to pinch myself looking back at the amazing experiences and moments I have had over the years and I realise how lucky I was to do a job that I love.

When I retired in May on a special and emotional night in Paris, it meant that I could take a step back and reflect on what I had achieved in the game and what it took to get there.

I didn't want to do another autobiography, instead I wanted to look at some of the images from my career and talk about what I was feeling at the time.

I really enjoyed doing this book, I hope you enjoy it too.

I realised one thing looking back at my career: it was never boring!

10

THERE ARE SO MANY

people I would like to thank here but I probably would need an entire second book to mention them.

I'm forever grateful for the love and support of Victoria, the boys and my little girl. Without them I couldn't and wouldn't have achieved what I have throughout my career and life. I love you so much.

I wouldn't be in this position today without my parents, grandparents and my sisters, Joanne and Lynne. They gave everything to help me realise my dreams. I will never forget their sacrifices.

Thanks also to Victoria's family: Jackie, Tony, Christian and Louise.

To my best mates, you know who you are and what you mean to me. You have made me laugh even in some of the most difficult moments. Thanks for your support.

I want to thank Simon Fuller for his invaluable advice and guidance over the years. May we have a long future working together.

To all the players, managers, coaches and staff who I have ever had the privilege and pleasure of working with, I want to say thank you. Football is truly a team sport and it was an honour to work with and play alongside you.

Finally, to the fans. In successful and hard times, you have always been there to support and pull me through. I will never forget that. Here's to many more new adventures together. We're only just beginning.

ENGLAND
PART ONE

LONDON

MANCHESTER

ENGLAND
PART TWO

MADRID

LOS ANGELES

MILAN

PARIS

ENGLAND

15

PART ONE

*Making my debut for my country was the
second proudest moment of my career.*

16   Always felt so emotional and proud
singing the national anthem.

18 *My first goal for England on my mum's birthday. I could just hear her saying: 'My boy did that for me.'*

(Overleaf)
I love this moment – celebrating with someone I'd known since I was 12 years old (Sol Campbell).

Big bear hug from Emile.
What a day for the whole team and
the country. Emile – gentle giant.

I COULD HEAR THE   23
banging of a drum. It was as if it was the only
sound in the world. Just one drum, banging out a
beat, the sound carrying directly onto the pitch.
The rest of the stadium seemed completely
silent, as if every single fan knew that the next
kick of the ball would decide the match.

Bang, bang; bang, bang; bang, bang.

Teddy Sheringham, my England team-mate,
tried to pick up the ball and place it on the spot
where Emile Heskey had been fouled by a Greek
defender a few moments earlier. I felt a rush of
adrenaline. The match was in the 93rd minute
and England were trailing 2–1. Unless we scored
now, we wouldn't qualify for the 2002 World Cup.

It didn't bear thinking about.

I grabbed the ball away from Teddy and
replaced it myself. He wasn't too keen on my
interference. He shoulder-barged me away, gently
but firmly. 'I've got this, David,' he said. 'I know I
can make it.'

But nothing was going to stop me taking that
free-kick. I felt confident, calm, certain. I knew

I could make it. I had missed a few already in the match, but my confidence was still sky high. I had tons of energy left, despite the fact it was in extra time.

'It's too far out for you, Teddy,' I said. 'Trust me. I've got it.'

I had done almost exactly the same thing as a teenager. We were having an A Team match in one of my first seasons at United. Bryan Robson, the United captain, was training with us because he was coming back from injury. We got a free-kick on the edge of the area and Robson stepped forward to take it.

He was also the England captain and one of the best players in the world, but I grabbed the ball off him. 'Sorry, but I usually take these,' I said. People couldn't believe my cheek. Robson gave me grief about it for years afterwards. But I think it demonstrated my confidence even as a youngster. I trusted in my ability to deliver.

Teddy could see that I was not going to back down and, even though he was older and wiser than me, he stepped away. It was just me, the ball, and the 25 yards separating me from the top left corner of the goal.

But this kick was not just about England; it was also about me. It was about drawing a line under four years of abuse. Four years of bitterness. Four years of England fans – not all of them, but enough to make it hurt – shouting the most horrible things at me while I was playing for my country.

Four years of pain.

I took two deep breaths, eyed the top corner of the net, and emptied my mind of everything except one thought: 'I am going to score.' There was a single focus: getting England into the World Cup finals. There was no doubt in my mind, no negativity. Just a sense of complete reassurance.

Confidence is a funny thing. People often say that you need a lot of luck to win. But, for me, confidence comes down to preparation. When you have practised something so much that it has become a part of who you are. Second nature. When you have done everything possible to give yourself the best chance.

I had taken lots of free-kicks over the years. Not just the free-kicks for Manchester United; not just the free-kicks that I took for the youth teams I played for growing up in East London. There were also the free-kicks I had taken in my back garden and at the local park with my dad, almost every one of them to send England into the World Cup finals or to win Manchester United the FA Cup.

I must have taken tens of thousands, maybe hundreds of thousands. I would go to the local park, place the ball on the ground, and aim at the wire meshing over the window of a small community hut. I would take 50, a hundred, I lost count of how many. The time just seemed to fly by. It didn't even seem like hard work.

When my dad got home from work, we would go over to the goal-posts together. He would stand between me and the goal, forcing me to bend the ball around him. People looking on must have thought we were mad. We kept going even when the sun had gone down, playing by the light coming out of the windows of the houses that surrounded the park. My legs would ache, but my dad always told me to keep going, to keep fighting, to keep striving.

I would carry on playing when I got home. I wasn't allowed a football in the house, so I would practise by kicking the Care Bears in my sister's bedroom. My mum thought it was funny, but it showed how much I loved football. I couldn't get enough of it. If you had given me the choice to skip school and play from morning till night, I would have jumped at the chance.

I guess when you have practised like that for twenty years, when you have put yourself on the line for so long, self-belief comes along as a by-product. You know you can do it because you have prepared to do it all your life. Michael Johnson, the legendary Olympic sprinter, once said: 'If you have done everything possible to prepare for your event, confidence will stick.' He is right.

And that is why I felt so confident stepping up to take that free-kick against Greece. It was as if all the years of commitment had prepared me for that one single moment.

Time seemed to slow down as I sized up the goal, hands on my hips. The drum was still beating and the tension was still rising.

I stepped slightly to the left and then began my run-up. I felt the ball on my boot and – in that strange way that sometimes happens in football – I knew instantly it was going into the back of the net.

There is something incredible when you strike a football in just the way you want to. It feels so satisfying, the tiny thud of the ball against your boot, and then the fizz of the ball as it speeds away. When you get it right, you hardly feel the impact. It is like kicking a feather.

As the ball flew towards the top left corner, before it had even hit the back of the net, I was off, sprinting towards the touch-line, shouting for joy. The silence had been replaced by a huge, almost deafening roar. The stadium just erupted. England were in the World Cup finals.

England were in the World Cup!

I jumped into the air and landed on both feet, then flung my arms backwards and embraced the crowd. It felt incredible to score the goal, but especially so at Old Trafford, a stadium that had become a home to me.

But I could sense something else, too. I had worked like crazy in that match. For some reason, I had endless reserves of energy. I ran, I tracked back, I tackled, I charged forward. Everything seemed possible. I was even trying things that I had never attempted before, and they kept coming off. People could see how much it meant to me to play for my country.

But the goal was the icing on the cake. It was as if all the lingering doubts about me as a player and as a person vanished in an instant. All of the pain, all of the bitterness, all of the hatred, all of the recriminations. I knew that one of the most difficult chapters in my life had come to an end.

I was forgiven at last.

I knew at this point it was a goal…

I look at this picture and it gives me
goosebumps. This is the moment
I felt the country had forgiven me.

30   *It doesn't get much better than this.*
Old Trafford… captain of my country…
93rd minute… one chance to go
through to the World Cup finals.

32   *I've never felt a reaction from a crowd*
      like the day that goal went in.

34   *Realising how important this goal was...*
    Nothing better than celebrating with your mate.

I know most of the nation wanted to kill me, but for the record my heart sank that day.

THREE AND A HALF

years earlier, things had been very different. It should have been a wonderful experience, playing for England in the 1998 World Cup. I was just 23 and it felt like the most exciting sporting opportunity of my life as I flew out with the squad to France.

Three weeks later, I was the most hated man in England.

It had started so well. Glenn Hoddle was the England manager and he had played me in all the matches in the build-up to the tournament. He had been a brilliant passer and I think he appreciated my ability to use the ball effectively. But the boss decided to drop me for the opening game. He obviously had his reasons, but it came as a huge shock.

It wasn't until the third match that I was given my chance to play. We had defeated Tunisia in our opener, but lost to Romania in our second game, during which I had come on as a substitute. It meant that we had to win the final group match against Colombia to qualify. It was a huge challenge, but I was up for it.

At our base in La Baule, we had a little training pitch where I could go out and practise on my own. The day before the Colombia game, I went down onto the pitch with a stereo, a CD of Tupac, the American rapper, and a big bag of balls. The temperature was ferociously hot, so I was just in shorts and a vest. But with the music blasting, I did what I had always done throughout my life. I practised.

I must have been down there for two hours at least, taking free-kicks, shaping the ball into the top corner, then shaping into the other corner, varying the distance, the direction, the speed of the ball, the shape of my body. I whacked the balls again and again, kicking them over and over until I had everything clear in my mind and felt that my body, boot and mind were in perfect harmony.

My confidence grew a little more.

It's a strange thing, but throughout my career I have suffered from a particular kind of criticism. I wonder if Hoddle had been influenced by it, which is why he dropped me for those first two matches. It was said that I am more interested in celebrity than application. That I spend more time in front of the mirror than on the training pitch. That clubs only sign me because they can sell replica shirts, not because I can help them to win matches.

I have always found this criticism difficult to take, because everything I have done, on and off the pitch, I have put my heart and soul into. I can be criticised for many things, perhaps, but not that. At my clubs, I would always try to arrive before everyone else and keep practising after everyone had left. I was not trying to please the coach, or be teacher's pet. It is just a part of who

I am. I had the same attitude when I played for England.

Maybe it was my dad and my mum who gave me such a ferocious work ethic. My dad is a gas fitter (he is still doing the job to this day) and I would watch him leaving for work at seven in the morning and coming home late at night. But he didn't stop grafting even then. As soon as he got home, he would come to the park with me and play football, coaching me till it got dark. He never let up. And he always seemed to enjoy it.

My mum has an incredible work ethic, too. She was a hairdresser and worked from morning until night. Then she came home and cooked for the family. Nothing ever seemed to be too much for either of them. No amount of hard graft ever phased them. They were not trying to influence me with their behaviour, but just by watching them, I was learning something about life.

If you want to make the best of yourself, if you want to reach your potential, you give it everything.

You never stop striving.

The day of the Colombia game was my mum's birthday, so I rang her up before the match for a chat and to wish her well. As ever, she was thinking about me.

'Score a goal for me, David,' she said.

In the event, I played a blinder. I passed well, got team-mates into good positions and, in the 29th minute, saw my big chance. Paul Ince was fouled as he ran towards the area with the ball. It was about 25 yards out, so a long way from goal. But it was just left of centre, the perfect place to shape a free-kick.

I hit it perfectly. All those hours of practice the day before, all the sweat, all the repetition, paid off. The goalkeeper made a desperate attempt to make up the ground to his right, but the ball was too fast, and the curve was too extreme. When it hit the back of the net, I sprinted over to the touch-line and celebrated with the England fans. It was my first goal for England. At the World Cup. On my mum's birthday.

No wonder I looked pleased.

We won 2–0 and my selection for the next match was a formality. A few days later, things got even better. Victoria was in America, touring with the Spice Girls. We spoke every day on the phone, but this call was different.

'I've got something to tell you,' she said.

I could tell from her voice that this was something important, something life-changing.

'Tell me please, quick,' I said.

'I am pregnant', she said.

I gasped. I felt my heart welling up. I was almost overwhelmed with joy. I had always wanted kids at a young age: I wanted my children to share my dreams, to share my life, to experience the world with me. I wanted to take them to training, to matches; I wanted them to know what my life was like as a footballer. I was so excited, I could hardly talk. This was huge.

I wanted to tell the world, but the Spice Girls were surrounded by secrecy at the time. They were so massive that everything about them was kept under wraps. So I promised not to tell any-one: not my friends in the England team, not my United buddies, not even my parents. Eventually they would find out. For now, the news was just for me and Victoria. And that was OK.

I turned my mind back to football. In two days' time, we faced Argentina in the knockout stages of the World Cup. It was a huge match,

partly because it was for a place in the quarter-finals, but also because of the history between the two nations. The newspapers were hyping it up and you could feel the growing excitement in the camp.

I thought of all the times I had watched the World Cup on the television. All the times I had dreamed of playing for England in the biggest competition in the world. All the times I had imagined walking out onto the pitch with the three lions on my shirt, the roar of the England fans in my ears, and the millions more watching on the television back home.

I felt like I was on form, in good physical shape, and was surging with confidence. The training sessions were going well. The manager seemed, for the time being at least, to be behind me. And my girlfriend, the woman of my dreams, was pregnant with our first child. It didn't get any better than this. Was it an omen?

The match started well. Alan Shearer scored a penalty in the 10th minute to equalise a spot kick by Gabriel Batistuta four minutes earlier. Then, just a few minutes later, I put the ball through to Michael Owen, who took it brilliantly in his stride, just inside the opposition half. From there, he swerved past the Argentinean defence like a slalom skier, before finessing the ball into the top corner.

It was a magnificent goal. We were on top. Even when they got one back with a cheeky free-kick just before half-time, it didn't stop our momentum. When we went in for the team-talk, everyone felt that this was ours for the taking. There was a real confidence within the team.

But two minutes into the second half, my world changed forever. I was standing in the centre of midfield when I got hit hard from behind by an Argentinean player. At the time I didn't know who it was. His knee went into my back and I was knocked flat onto the pitch. As he got up from on top of me, I felt his hand going towards the top of my head, and then tugging at my hair. Then he patted me on my head.

My reaction was as quick as it was stupid. I knew he was behind me, walking backwards, so I swung my leg up towards him. My foot probably travelled no more than a couple of feet, but the consequences would reverberate for the next four years. As I got up I could see that it was Diego Simeone, and that he had collapsed in a heap the moment my foot made contact with his leg. I knew that he was exaggerating – I hardly caught him – but I also knew I had made a terrible, disastrous mistake.

I wished I could have taken it back. I wished I had thought a bit more about the consequences before reacting to his provocation. I wished I could just get on with the game, with a hand-shake and an apology. But it was too late. I knew what was going to happen. I could see the referee beckoning me over and from his expression, I knew I was finished.

As the referee raised the red card into the air, I felt my stomach turn to ice. I found it difficult to control my features. It felt like the world had turned inside out. I didn't blame the referee – I had given him no choice. I turned around and began the walk back to the dressing room.

It was probably the longest walk in my life. The distance was no more than 80 yards from the half-way line back to the changing rooms, but those minutes felt like an eternity. Looking back, I am not sure what thoughts were going through my mind: it was a swirl of fear, guilt, anger, worry and confusion. My head was spinning. It was impossible to take in.

I had been given a red card for England at the World Cup finals. It could cost us the match.

Terry Byrne, the masseur, put his arm around my shoulders as I walked into the dressing room. The rules stated that I had to stay in there for the remainder of the match. I texted Victoria and asked her if she had seen what had happened. She replied straight away to say that, watching on television out in America, it didn't seem as if I had done much wrong. That was reassuring to hear, although, to be fair, she was not a football expert.

It was a strange place to be: thoughts racing through my head, astonishment that the dream had turned into a nightmare, fear that we might end up losing the match and that I would forever feel responsible. The seconds ticked by. Every moment seemed heavy. I was pretty much alone – only Terry Byrne was with me – but it was as if the room was overflowing with tension.

I took a long, long shower. Perhaps I thought that I could wash away what had happened with soap and water. Afterwards, I crept out into the tunnel to watch extra-time. It was like torture as the match ticked towards penalties. When David Batty missed his spot-kick, it was all over. The dream was finished. We would be flying home tomorrow. England were out of the World Cup.

When the England players came back into the dressing room, nobody breathed a word to me. There was almost complete silence. I could feel my stomach tightening even more. I gulped, breathed in, and gulped again.

I was in a packed changing room, but I had never felt so lonely in my life. I was isolated and afraid. Only Gary and Scholesey came over to give me a word or two of comfort. I didn't know where to look. I didn't know what to say. I wanted to shout out how sorry I was, how much I wanted to take it back, but it was too late. I was trapped in my own sense of guilt and anxiety.

Then, as if from nowhere, a totally unexpected crumb of comfort: Tony Adams put his arm around me. It was a strong embrace. I could feel that he meant it; that he could see how much I was suffering; that he wanted to take away some of the pain. 'Look son, everyone makes mistakes,' he said. 'Don't let it get you down. You are going to come back stronger and better.'

I wanted to hold onto him longer, or at least to tell him how much that sturdy embrace and those heartfelt words of wisdom meant to me. But I guess I was too young. It was a lesson in leadership. He wasn't the captain of the England team at that time, he didn't have any particular responsibility to look out for the young players. But he was a leader of men. He was a role model.

I have never forgotten those words, or the example he set. Tony Adams is one in a million. I will always appreciate that gesture.

When we went out to the team coach, I caught sight of my parents. They were standing there, looking over at me, concern etched across their faces. They had been coming to matches since I was a kid. They had made so many sacrifices, had driven up and down the country endlessly to be with me, had often given up their own ambitions to help me achieve mine.

I knew how proud they were of me, and how much it meant to them that I had made it into the England team. And I knew how much they were hurting, too, now that I had been sent off. There was no blame, no sense of anger. There was only love. I felt myself welling up. Almost before I had reached my dad, I was sobbing. He grabbed hold of me, pulled me tight, as I let everything out.

I was shaking almost uncontrollably. I was 23 years of age, but I was crying like a baby, clinging on to the shoulders of my dad as if he was a lifeline in a raging sea.

Twenty yards away, the Argentineans were celebrating in their team bus. I could hear their shouting and singing as their bus bounced up and down. Many of them were swirling their shirts above their heads, banging the windows. I didn't blame them. They had won a huge match. They deserved their celebrations.

But there I was, distraught. I didn't want to leave my parents. I needed their support. I could tell that they wanted to stay with me. I could see how worried they were. But after a few minutes, I was called to the team bus to take the trip back to the hotel.

I played snooker that night until the early hours with Steve McManaman, Terry Byrne and Steve Slattery, with a couple of beers to numb the pain. I knew that the reaction back home would be bad. People would probably blame me for the defeat. Football is a huge sport and you have to expect criticism from time to time.

But nothing could possibly have prepared me for what was about to happen.

I got a taste, a little flavour, when I arrived back at Heathrow. We landed as a team, but I was flying straight out to the States to spend a couple of weeks with Victoria. As we got into the terminal, somebody from the airport special services told me that there were a couple of cameras waiting for me.

But the cameras followed me through the terminal when I left the England team to make my way to my next flight. As I walked, looking ahead, trying to hold onto my composure, this horrible journalist kept digging at me. Winding me up, trying to get me to react, riling me over and over again. It was awful.

'How does it feel to let your country down? How does it feel to let your family down? How does it feel to let your team-mates down?'

I couldn't believe what was happening. I didn't know what to say. I just kept my head down, praying that I would get to the lounge as soon as possible. The journalist kept it up all the way there. He was merciless; he almost seemed to be enjoying it. When I got to the lounge, I went straight to the bathroom and cried again. I couldn't get my head around it.

Was this going to keep on happening? Was this what life was going to be like?

It was lovely to spend time with Victoria in the States and to get some respite from everything that was going on back home, particularly because it gave us a chance to talk about our baby. It was just what I needed. She is so good at taking my mind off things.

But when I got back to Manchester, the full extent of the nightmare hit home. There were death threats. Bullets hand-delivered through the post. My effigy burned from a lamppost. It was complete madness, but it was really happening.

It was really happening.

One newspaper turned my face into a dartboard. With all the terrible things happening in the world, the editor seemed to think that the biggest villain was a footballer who had got sent off in a match in Saint-Étienne. The dartboard was probably his idea of a joke. But on top of everything else that was going on, it just seemed like another piece of the nightmare.

It was relentless. When I stopped to fill up at petrol stations, people would berate me. When I pulled up at traffic lights, I would get abusive hand gestures. When Manchester United went to play the first away match of the season at Upton Park, I had to be escorted into the ground under armed guard.

After that match, against West Ham, I looked at the photos of people screaming abuse at me while I was taken into the stadium by a seven-foot-tall policeman. I was amazed by the anger. Their faces were red, contorted, the veins standing out on their necks.

This was not good-natured teasing. It was not harmless banter. It was full-on hatred. And it scared me. What with the threats of violence that were being sent to me through the post, it really scared me.

I got booed by away fans for an entire season. Every time I got the ball, it would start, thousands of people screaming, shouting, singing the most vile songs about my family. At one ground, it was almost deafening. Grown men, often with their children in tow, were swearing and cursing about someone they had never met, and couldn't possibly judge.

One night at my home in Manchester, I was woken by a huge noise. My two Rottweiler puppies were going crazy. They lived in a little kennel in the garden. So I went down and looked out of the window. Outside, there was a guy just looking up at me. The lights from the house were on him, but he was not trying to hide. He wanted me to see him and him to see me. He wanted to scare the living daylights out of me.

He just kept staring up, his eyes not seeming to flicker. I stood there for a minute, almost as if I had been hypnotised, and I thought: surely he is going to go at some point. But he stood there for five minutes. He didn't blink. He didn't budge. I called the police, but by the time they arrived he had vanished. They couldn't find him.

I just wanted to know one thing: when was this nightmare going to end?

The worst thing of all was the effect it had on my family. My grandad would phone up and say that someone had approached him and been abusive. He would get hassled for interviews. People would shout at him on the streets. It was non-stop. It was one thing for the press to come after me, but it was reprehensible to go after my grandparents, my parents, and others close to me. That was the most painful thing of all. The incident in Saint-Étienne was not just threatening to ruin my life, but those of my loved ones, too.

But there was one positive to come out of the World Cup incident. One silver lining. One thing that helped me to keep going and to believe that one day I would come through it.

It was the reaction of Manchester United. The reaction of the manager, my team-mates and, most of all, the United supporters. They backed me to the hilt. The more the animosity grew, the more they held out against it. The more people screamed abuse at me, the more they chanted my name from the terraces. That was

United through and through. That is what the club was about.

That is why it is the greatest club in the world.

The morning after the match against Argentina, the fight-back had already begun. Alex Ferguson phoned me up. He got straight to the point. 'Don't worry son,' he said. 'Things have happened, but it is over now. You are a Manchester United player. We will look after you. Have a few weeks' holiday and remember that when you get back, you will have the support of everyone. We will protect you.'

That is how things work at United. When things happen outside the club, everything closes around you. Everyone protects you. Nothing gets in, nothing gets out. The manager puts his arm around you even if you are in the wrong. He will never let anyone give any of the United players abuse. He will be the one to tell you to your face, but outside the club he will never criticise any player.

Hoddle was different. It wasn't until a long time afterwards that I saw the interview he had given after the match. I liked Hoddle, respected him. But I found this interview difficult to take. He didn't blame me, exactly, but he made it clear that he thought that my mistake cost England the game. He showed his anger and irritation with me. It definitely fed the frenzy.

At United, on the other hand, it felt like a blanket had been placed around me. Photographers were kept in the distance at The Cliff training ground. My team-mates had my back. And the United fans were just fantastic. They cheered me, made me feel loved, from the first match of the season until the last. It was incredible to have thousands of fans on my side, just as everyone else had turned against me. They were a rock.

The 1998–99 season was the most incredible in my career. I will return to it later in the book. It was the season of the Treble, the miracle of the Nou Camp, the season of that incredible FA Cup semi-final replay against Arsenal. But, for me, it has always been about something more than that. It was the season when I lived a nightmare and a dream at the same time. It felt like two stories happening all at once. But the dream won out in the end.

I am often asked: How is it possible to play to your top level when people are baying for your blood? How was it possible to have one of my best seasons amid all that abuse? Well, the United faithful helped hugely. They were massive and it makes me feel proud to look back on how genuinely supportive they were. The boss and my team-mates helped, too. They were incredible, in the dressing room, on the pitch, everywhere. We had an unbreakable spirit.

But even with all that support, it was still tough and there were moments when I felt my heart trembling. I remember the opening game against Leicester. I had a free-kick in the last minute when we were trailing 2–1. My stomach tightened, because this was a huge moment. I had been booed by the away supporters throughout the match, but the United fans had drowned them out a lot of the time. I had taken one corner, and the Reds had all stood up and just chanted my name.

It was only as I stepped up to take the free-kick that I felt my willpower hardening. It would have been easy to be negative, to worry about the consequences, but I just felt that little bit of steel

inside. Partly, it was the extraordinary support I had received. But it was also all the practice over the years: the thousands of free-kicks I had taken in rain, sleet and snow. It gave me confidence.

As the ball left my boot, I could see it had a chance. It wasn't a perfect strike, but it was good enough. The ball slipped in under the keeper and, as the crowd rose to its feet and the United faithful roared again, I felt this huge sense of relief. It was just the shot in the arm I needed. My doubts seemed to vanish right there. I was euphoric.

Afterwards, I watched the match on the television. I remember looking at the boss and his face showed just how proud he was. It was like his own son had scored. He was thrilled. That meant so much to me because it showed just how tight-knit we were as a club. The boss knew how much confidence it would give me.

The other thing I always remember was the reaction of Roy Keane. He is a tough guy. He rarely shows his emotions, unless it is to tear strips off you. But he came running over and I could see in his eyes how much that goal meant to him. In some ways, Keane's reaction has always meant more to me than the goal itself. I have always treasured that.

By the end of an incredible season, United had won the Treble, the first English club ever to do so. I had played in almost every match and scored some vital goals. At FIFA's World Player Awards, voted for by coaches and captains of national teams, I was ranked second in the world, behind Rivaldo of Brazil and Barcelona, and ahead of Shevchenko, Batistuta, Veron, Figo, Keane and Raul.

For me, it was an honour just to be mentioned in the same breath as those guys.

The lessons were painful, but I learned a lot that year. I learned that when you are in the public eye, things can get out of control so quickly that it leaves your head spinning. I learned that when you are at the centre of a feeding frenzy, you desperately need support – and I had it in spades: from United, from the fans, from my family, from Victoria.

I also learned that when things go wrong in life – as they always will at some stage, no matter how hard you try – you can't allow them to defeat you. You have to be strong, to stand tall, to look deep inside and find a willingness to carry on. It is not easy. I don't pretend that it is. Many people face difficulties that make football seem trivial. But we should never underestimate ourselves. The human spirit is incredibly powerful if you give it a chance.

For me, the nightmare that started with that kick out at Diego Simeone on a small rectangle of turf in Saint-Étienne only truly ended three and a half years later at Old Trafford in that World Cup qualifier against Greece. Throughout that time, despite the trophies and the accolades, I could still feel the lingering animosity from a certain group of England fans. When I played for my country, there was the sense that supporters had their doubts about me. You could feel it in the atmosphere.

It didn't even change when I was made England captain by Peter Taylor, when he became caretaker manager. It was a huge honour and something I had always wanted, but the hatred continued to linger. Even when Sven-Göran Eriksson told me that I would be keeping the armband when he became England manager, the abuse continued. I still felt that I had to

convince a significant minority of England fans that I was not the person they thought I was.

On the morning of the Greece game, I knew that the match was not going to be easy. There was something telling me that this was going to be a tough game, a hard-fought game, despite the predictions that we would walk all over them. The sun was beating down and it was incredibly hot. As we walked out to the bus, I looked around and could tell that everyone was apprehensive. The players, the support staff, the manager.

When the match started, Greece found their feet almost immediately. They were oozing confidence. They scored in the 36th minute, stunning the crowd into silence. It felt a little ominous. We couldn't quite find our range or rhythm, however much we tried. It wasn't until the 68th minute that we equalised. You could almost hear the relief in the stadium. I chipped a ball through to Teddy (he had come on as a substitute), who flicked it into the goal.

But then, as if in a nightmare, Greece scored again and our fans became subdued once more.

As the clock ticked down, it looked desperate for us. The tempo in our team was not right. At Old Trafford, the pitch is always wet, because they hit it with sprinklers before the match. But the temperature was so hot against Greece that the pitch was bone dry. The ball was not rolling as slickly as it should have been. Our rhythm, which had never been right throughout the match, was in danger of disappearing altogether.

When Teddy was fouled outside the area in the dying moments, it was our last chance. Qualification hinged on one kick of the ball. This was an opportunity for me to score, but it was also a chance to draw a line, once and for all, under all the pain from 1998. That is why I took the ball from Teddy. That is why I celebrated so wildly when I scored.

I should have been absolutely knackered because of the number of miles I had run in that game. More than any I had run in any game before in my life. More than I thought my lungs could cope with. But, at that moment, I could have run the length of the pitch.

The nightmare had finally ended.

I knew the moment I kicked out I was off...
I felt physically sick.

50 *I could feel the disappointment in Alan's reaction. But Scholesy's look was one you would get from a family member.*

52   *I'll never get over how I felt that night.*
    Longest walk of my life.

RIDGEWAY ROVERS UNDER II 1985-1986

STEVE KIRBY (COACH), STUART UNDERWOOD (MANAGER), TED BECKHAM (ASST. COACH)
CHRIS DAY, DANNY FIELDER, GLEN SUTTON, ELIOT WYKES, NICKY LOCKWOOD, CRAIG LLOYD, JOEL SWAIN, JASSON BRISSET.
RITCHIE SUTTON, ROBERT UNDERWOOD, RYAN KIRBY, MATTHEW BARHAM, DAVE BECKHAM.

LONDON

(Previous page)
The hut behind is where I practised my accuracy, I used to aim the ball at the cage around the window.

The start of my football career. 59

Not sure about my dad's moustache…

Growing up with two sisters was always interesting...

My dad's hero; mine too.

MANCHESTER

68 *My dad and me with Sir Matt Busby.*
A very early memory of Manchester
United was the smell of Sir Matt's
pipe as I walked past his office.

With my mum in the changing rooms.

MY DAD IS A TOUGH

man. Tough but fair. He was the person who got me to support Manchester United as a young boy. He loves United, worships them almost, so when I was old enough to take an interest in football, there was only one option. I fell in love with the club before I can even remember.

I loved United, and I loved football, too. I practised every day, kicking the ball up against the wall in the back garden, or doing keep-me-ups, or booting the ball as hard as I could into the fence. Then, when he got home from work, I would go down to the field around the corner with Dad, which is when the real hard graft would begin.

My dad was as hard as nails when we practised together, encouraging me to use both feet, learning about the first touch, taking free-kicks till my legs hurt. He was a decent player – he once had trials for Leyton Orient – and he understood the basics really well. He didn't want me to have all the flash skills, without being able to trap the ball, or use my left foot, or control an incoming pass.

Sometimes, he raised his voice if I was doing things wrong, or he thought I was being lazy. Occasionally, he shouted. But he always had my best interests at heart. He would have done anything to help me. I knew that. That is why I never resented his toughness.

We were incredibly close as a family. In many ways, it was a perfect combination, because my dad was a bit of a taskmaster while my mum was gentle and caring. She was much softer in her character. She worked as hard as my dad, and made as many sacrifices, but she showed her love in a different way. They were, and are, in their different ways, terrific parents.

It was my mum who drove me to the match that changed everything. I was playing for Waltham Forest, my district side, against Redbridge as a 12-year-old. I played really well. Almost every time I got on the ball, I made something happen. Afterwards, as we were walking to the car, my mum looked at me with a smile on her face.

'Lucky you had a good game today,' she said.
'Why?'

'A Manchester United scout is over there. He was watching you today. He was impressed.'

I burst out crying. Playing for United had been my dream since before I could remember. I had worried about whether anyone from the club would ever see me play down in London. I didn't think their scouts travelled that far afield. I used to go to bed at night fretting about whether the club that surrounded me, in posters and on my official United bedcover, would ever discover the little boy from East London who dreamed of playing at Old Trafford.

I loved United so much as a kid that my family had paid for me to go up to Manchester to the Bobby Charlton Soccer School when I was 10 and then again when I was 11. In the second year I had won a skills competition at the camp and had been presented with a prize at Old Trafford, something that filled Dad with pride. He couldn't stop grinning when I went up to Bobby Charlton himself to collect the trophy.

But it was that match against Redbridge that changed everything. I was invited up to United for a few trials and I did everything I could to impress the staff. I loved being up there, even if I was a little homesick. The coaches seemed to like the way I played and they liked my attitude. Then, a few weeks after I got back, Alex Ferguson phoned our home. My dad almost dropped the receiver.

'We think David has a lot of ability and a really good character. We want to sign him for United.'

I was too excited to sleep. It was like crossing a threshold to a new life. For the first two years, while I was still at school in London, I would go up to train at United two or three times a year during the holidays and then for six full weeks during the summer. We stayed in a concrete block in Salford and trained on United's second ground at Littleton Road. The rest of the time I was training and playing matches in London.

When I was fifteen and a half, the big day arrived to move up to Manchester for good as a YTS trainee. My mum cried and I did a bit, too.

My eyes were as wide as saucers as we travelled up. The plan was for me to stay in digs with one of the families who put up the youth team players. My parents assured me that they would come to visit every weekend and travel up for every single game. I knew I could take them at their word. Their commitment was never in doubt.

For the first few months, I really missed home. It was a long way from my family and I took a while to find my feet. But when I moved in with Tommie and Annie, a lovely couple whose home was just a few yards from the entrance to The Cliff, I finally settled. It was a home from home. They were wonderful in so many ways: caring, loyal, accepting, decent. They had a lovely baby daughter, who I used to watch television with, sitting on my single bed. The home-cooked food was fantastic, too.

The training at The Cliff was tough. The coach was Eric Harrison, a straight-talking and rather scary Yorkshireman. He barked and he growled, and the lads were terrified of him, but we also knew that he was honest, straightforward, and completely committed to United. We hung on his every word, whether he was talking about football or life. And he liked us, too, for one simple reason. No matter how much training we did, we were ready to do more. Much more.

The incredible thing about that generation of lads, who came into the youth team with me in 1991, is that they were as committed to hard training as I ever was. We couldn't get enough of it. Perhaps it was our family backgrounds. Gary and Phil Neville had a dad whose basic motto was 'give it everything and you will reap the rewards'. At the end of practice, while most of the older lads were sitting in the canteen with their feet up, Gary was still pounding the ball against the wall.

He never tired. He never seemed to lose his motivation. Even when we were knackered, our legs heavy as blocks of steel, he still had his eyes on the prize. In our first week at The Cliff, Eric told us that only 1 per cent of youth players make it into the first team. It was a stern but important warning. He made us understand that although we had made it into the United youth team, we had made only one tiny step on the road to top-flight football.

Gary took Eric at his word. He had football at the forefront of his mind in every single thing he did: what time he went to bed, every detail of his preparation, and all his extra practice. The others were pretty much the same. Scholesey, Giggsy, Nicky Butt: they wanted it so much. They were an incredible influence on me.

I already had a strong work ethic because of my family background. Practice was like second nature. But with these guys around, I knew that I had to take it to another level, to put in the extra shifts, to leave nothing to chance. We had to show commitment like never before if we were going to make it into the United first team. And that is exactly what we did.

We came back in the evenings for extra practice with the Under-15s, we trained during lunchtimes, we ran until we couldn't run any more. The older boys thought we were swots, teacher's pets, and gave us quite a bit of abuse, but we weren't bothered. The more we practised, the better we became. Soon, we were overtaking the older boys who were realising, a little too late, that they had taken things too easy. This was payback of a kind, although we didn't really see it that way. We were just doing our jobs.

It wasn't just the quantity of extra practice. Gary, in particular, was incredibly focussed on quality. He was always trying to do things better, practising his crosses, honing his accuracy, kicking the ball against the wall until he had everything just right. His concentration was incredible. We loved the training because we wanted to put our hearts and souls into football. This is what we lived for. Harrison loved our attitude. We even saw him smile a few times.

I guess all this was about more than football; it was, in many ways, an attitude to life. I have always believed that life is about giving it your all. If you do that, if you do something with all your heart, you can look back knowing that you did everything possible to achieve your dreams. It doesn't mean that you will always get everything you want. It doesn't mean there will never be hard times. But it does mean that you will reach your potential. And isn't there something amazing about that thought? And your potential is often far higher than you might think.

By the end of our first season at United, the 'Class of 92' was improving so rapidly that fans started coming down to watch our matches. We were progressing through the FA Youth Cup and the press became interested, too. Bringing through young players was a big deal at the club, part of the tradition laid down by Sir Matt Busby. The Babes and the Munich air disaster were still talked about around The Cliff. People started speculating about a new generation threatening to break into the first team. We could hardly believe what we were hearing.

The first team! The Manchester United first team!

Could this be happening?

Alex Ferguson was always at the training ground keeping an eye on things. He was like a force-field: visible when he was present, but still exerting an influence even when he was somewhere else. We feared him and respected him in about equal measure. He had a ferocious temper, but a real sense of the importance of nurturing talent. We were confident that if we delivered, he would back us.

Then, on 15th May 1992, we won the FA Youth Cup against Crystal Palace. It was an incredible feeling because United hadn't won it for years. To do it at Old Trafford made it even sweeter. The future looked bright. Even Eric said so. The transition to first team football was on the horizon.

We were about to make our great leap forward.

Being in the same team as Giggsy and winning the FA Youth Cup with him was inspirational – it showed us where we could get to with hard work.

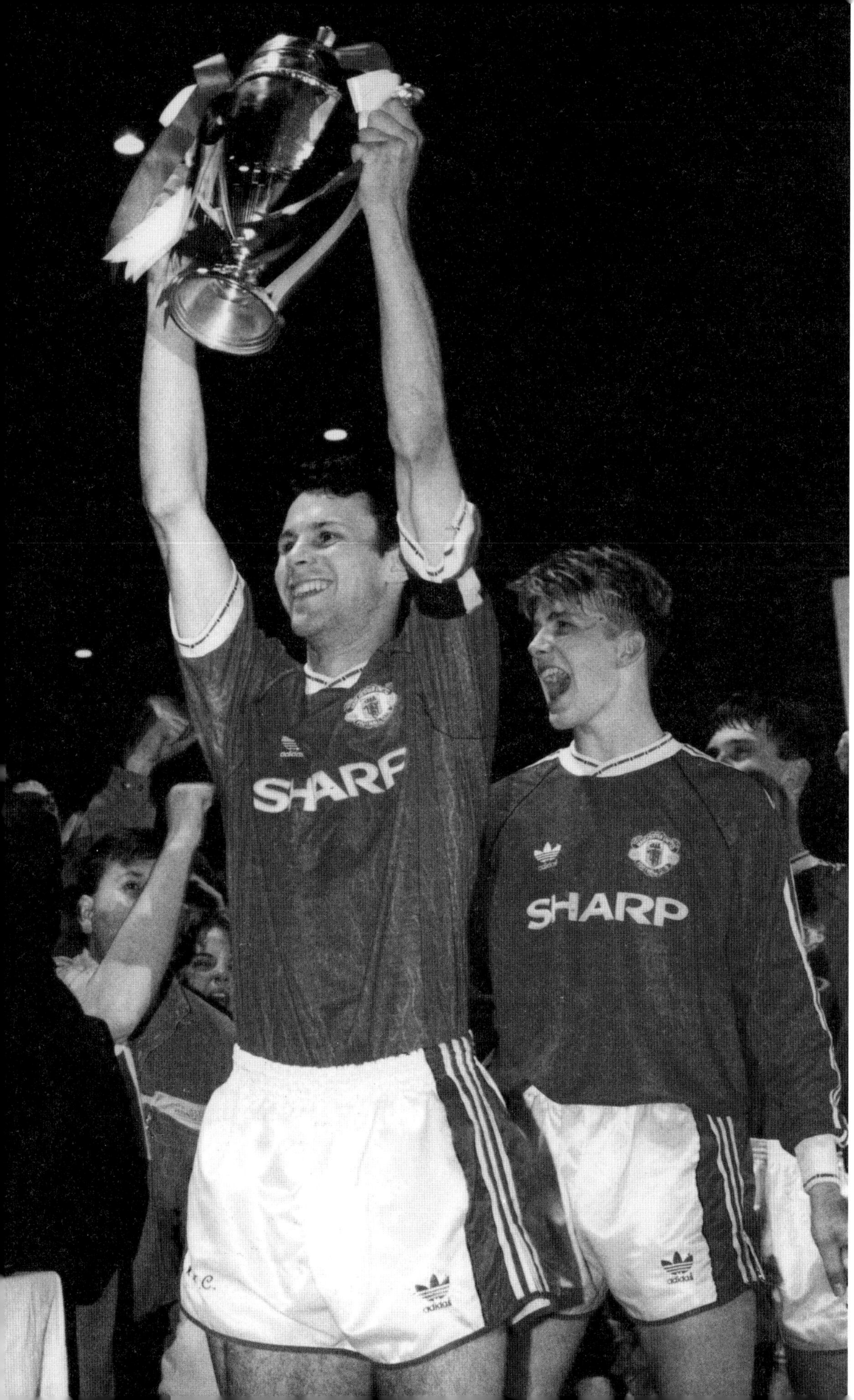
SHARP
SHARP

One of my best memories at United.

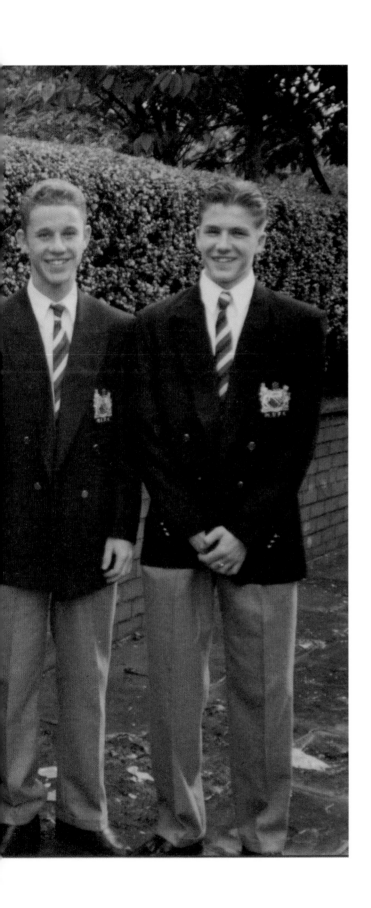

So proud to wear this blazer. 79

80   *Eric Harrison and*
             the 'Class of 92.'

82   *"David, you're lucky that
       went in or you were off."*

Running to celebrate with the fans.
It didn't happen that often,
but I loved scoring.

WE ALL SAW THE headlines. How could you miss them? It was everywhere. Fergie had lost the plot. He had sold the heart of the team. He had put a bunch of wide-eyed kids in the starting line-up, who may have been good in youth competitions, but had no chance of cutting it in the toughest, fiercest, most competitive league on the planet.

There were articles about it, debates on the radio, polls in newspapers. People had already criticised the boss for selling Paul Ince and Andrei Kanchelskis. Even I thought he was crazy to sell Mark Hughes, who I had always worshipped as a player. But after the first match of the season, even a few United supporters were having doubts about putting me, Gary and Paul in the squad.

Alan Hansen summed it all up on *Match of the Day*: 'You can't win anything with kids'.

I watched *Match of the Day* that night after getting back from the match at Villa Park on 19th August 1995. The dream seemed to be vanishing before our very eyes. The young lads who had come through the academy had always dreamed of playing for United in the first team. Not just as optional extras, but as players who could win trophies for the club we had supported growing up.

Gary Neville, Paul Scholes, Philip Neville, Ryan Giggs and Nicky Butt had become more than just team-mates; we were friends. We were brothers in arms.

When three of us were selected for the opening match of the season, the excitement was beyond words. This showed that the gaffer believed in us, thought we could do a job for him, could maybe even help to take United to the title. It all seemed to suddenly make sense. Kanchelskis had been sold because the boss thought he had, in me, a right-sided replacement. The same logic applied to the other big sales. It made us feel ten feet tall. We were being groomed for stardom.

Then there came the trip to Villa Park. I came on from the bench in the second half, but by that time it was too late. I thought I played pretty well, scoring a goal after 84 minutes, but I got a mouthful from the boss in the dressing room afterwards for tearing around the pitch, abandoning my position. It hurt, but I knew that he was probably right. Even worse, though, was the feeling that confronted us youngsters as we drove home.

Is this a step too far? Are we really up to the job?

By the time we arrived at West Ham for the next game, however, we had turned it around in our minds. We all had that little bit of steel; we felt that we had worked too hard to let it all slip away just as the adventure was really taking off. We had some brilliant older players alongside us, too; people who had done it all before. The likes of Steve Bruce, Gary Pallister and Peter Schmeichel. They helped just by being there, with their calmness and confidence. The dressing room was quiet but determined.

We went out and beat West Ham 2–1 in the second match of the season. It was the beginning of a five-match winning sequence. By the end of it, all those early doubts had vanished. In some ways, they seemed silly. I scored the winner against Blackburn in the fourth match of the season, then we beat Everton and Bolton. We were on a roll.

Manchester United is an extraordinary football club. It is extraordinary because of the history, the fans and the stadium. It is extraordinary because, in Sir Matt Busby and Sir Alex Ferguson, it has had two of the greatest managers who ever lived. But it is also special because it has a sense of magic. You can feel it everywhere. A sense that you are at the centre of the footballing world.

That season, it felt like we were surrounded by magic. Every now and again I had to pinch myself. I was starting matches, helping to win matches; I was sitting in the dressing room alongside club legends, listing to team-talks from Alex Ferguson; playing in a team alongside guys I had spent three years with in the youth team. Guys who had become close friends. I had bought my own house in Worsley, living next door to Ryan Giggs. I had my own car.

Could it get any better?

As the season progressed, we grew in confidence. We were beating teams, sometimes comfortably, but we wanted more. We were training hard, loving the fact that our labours were leading to tangible results, and making headlines. We were chasing Newcastle in the league, but they were very much in our sights as the season moved towards the run-in. We knew we could haul them in. What's more, we were also in the FA Cup semi-finals.

After that crushing defeat against Aston Villa in our first match, we were now looking at the possibility of the Double. Every time we won, I would look up into the stands and wave to my parents, who travelled everywhere to watch me in action. It was so special, being able to give something back. To see their pleasure in what I was achieving.

There was something else, too. I was playing alongside Eric Cantona and that was thrilling in itself. He had come back into the team in the first week of October 1995 after serving a seven-month ban for kicking a fan at Selhurst Park the previous April. He had also done community service as part of his sentence. He stayed with us throughout his ban, training with the team, but on 6th October he made his comeback. In characteristic fashion, he scored.

Cantona was an incredible player. He was the linchpin of almost everything we did once he made his return. His work-rate in training was phenomenal: he just kept going, practising the simple things over and over. Then he would get into his tiny, unpretentious car and drive home. It was a revelation to see someone, who looked so naturally gifted, demonstrating a work ethic that took the breath away.

On the pitch, he was immense. He could do everything. He almost always reserved his finest performances for the crunch games, making the crucial difference between winning and losing.

To play alongside him was an education in the art of playing football, in just how hard you have to work to fulfil your potential, and in how you can be an individual and a team player at the same time. I think even the boss learned from his example.

Towards the end of the season, with Eric in our midst, we were pretty much unstoppable. In the second to last match, against Nottingham Forest, I scored twice. Scholesy and Giggsy scored, too, and so did Eric. It was a 5–0 drubbing, but it could have been more. When we defeated Middlesbrough 3–0 in the last match of the season, we were champions. We had done it. United had won the league – with kids.

But there was no time for a big celebration. Six days later, we had the FA Cup final. This was the showpiece match that all of us had grown up fantasising about, and now we were going to be playing at Wembley, beneath the twin towers, in our first season as first team players at Manchester United, the best club in the world, having already won the Premier League.

I just wanted to know who was writing the script.

Liverpool were our opponents, and they showed up for the traditional pre-match walk around Wembley in cream Armani suits and white Gucci shoes. It was one of the most memorable matches I have played in. The action was a little sticky. Midway through the second half, it didn't look as if either team would score. Then we got a corner and I ran down to take it, steadying myself for a big moment. I swung it in, a yard outside the six-yard box. David James fumbled it and it fell to Eric Cantona. His volley was a peach.

It turned out to be the decisive goal. We had won the Double.

I felt a rush as powerful, as overwhelming, as anything I had ever experienced on a football field, before or since. It was almost too much to take in. As we went up the steps to collect our medals, I remember turning to Gary Neville: 'Can you believe this is happening?' I said. He was as dazed as I was. From the opening game, when so many doubted us, to now, when we were on top of the world, was a rollercoaster that just made your head spin.

We celebrated like crazy in the dressing room and the club arranged a celebration dinner in Manchester. It was fantastic to spend those precious evenings with my team-mates and also my parents, who were there as always. But there was also something else in the atmosphere. This was United. There was no time for resting on our laurels.

We had to be ready to go again the next season.

That is another magical thing about United: a relentless appetite for success. It starts with the manager, but everyone in the club comes to buy into it. Success is not expected; it is demanded. You have to be prepared to play your best ever match, have your best ever season, and then attempt to exceed it. You are always looking towards the next summit.

We had won the Double.

But could we ever go one better?

First full game for United in the Champions League. What a night. 4–0. I mishit a shot that went in. The best moment was celebrating with Eric... I got the feeling he was proud of us that night.

I vividly recall sitting with players like Eric eating beans on toast for our pre-match meal.

92   *Cantona saying 'What a goal'*
        was better than scoring this.

94   *The reaction of Eric and the boss*
        made this goal special for me.

Always nice giving big Dave Seaman the eyes…

Sorry Dave.
Loved scoring against the Arsenal.

Being carried off the
pitch after beating
Arsenal thanks to
Giggsy's amazing solo
goal. I scored a pretty
good goal that day as
well.

I remember someone
tried to take my boots
off too.

102 *This sums up the commitment and togetherness we had as a team. I love Jaap's face in this picture.*

What a season… for both of us. Yorkie never played without a smile on his face.

I RAN UP THE PITCH

to take the corner, willing my legs forward, hoping that we might finally catch a break. I was not optimistic, to be honest. The game had been sapping, we had never really found our tempo. Bayern Munich deserved to be ahead.

But we were not out of it yet. We still believed the impossible might happen as the clock ticked into extra time. I looked around the pitch, at Butty, Ryan, Gaz and the rest. They still believed, too. The unbreakable spirit that had carried us to the edge of history was still alive.

We had to score now, or the Treble was over.

The 1998–99 season was the most intense, memorable, astonishing season of football I have ever been involved in. Perhaps it is not an exaggeration to say that it was the most remarkable season in English football history.

It was not just the fact that when we travelled to Barcelona to play in the Champions League final we were on the verge of winning an unprecedented three trophies. It was not just the fact that United and the gaffer craved the

European title so much, following in the steps of Busby. More than anything, it was the way we did it, the matches we had to come through on the road to the ultimate prize.

For me, of course, there was another dimension: all the abuse that came my way because of the sending off against Argentina, and all the support that United fans had given me as a consequence. My emotions would have been intense whatever happened that season. But with our assault on three trophies, it was out of this world. As we approached the end of the season, every match was an epic.

Matches like the Arsenal FA Cup semi-final replay at Villa Park, when we went down to ten men but refused to surrender, Peter Schmeichel saving a penalty from Dennis Bergkamp in the dying moments before Giggsy sprinted half the length of the pitch, snaking past four defenders before shooting into the roof of the net. All these years on, I still regard that as the single most amazing match I ever took part in.

Then there was the Champions League semi-final second leg against Juventus, when we went 2–0 down and looked doomed. The fight-back was almost beyond belief: the headed goal by Keane, the equaliser by Yorke and then, six minutes from the end, the winning effort by Andy Cole, which took us into the final. Even then we couldn't celebrate after the match. There was too much at stake.

In those last few weeks, it seemed like every match was a cup final. Every match either took us one step closer to a dream that few people believed possible, or it extinguished the dream altogether. We all wanted to keep playing, keep winning, even as our legs were giving out. It was

as if all the training, all the extra practice, all the fitness work, came together to see us through.

The last match of the Premier League season, which we had to win to guarantee the league title, was tougher than anyone expected. Spurs were up for it (despite predictions they would just roll over to deny Arsenal the title). Les Ferdinand scored for the visitors before I put things level by beating David Seaman from 25 yards. My celebrations showed how much we wanted it, all fist pumping and aggression. Andy Cole, who had come on as substitute, scored in the second half and we clung on till the end. We had won the league.

In any normal season, it would have been a moment for huge celebrations. It would have been a moment to reflect upon all the hard work it had taken to lift the trophy. But we couldn't celebrate for an instant.

The FA Cup final at Wembley was just a few days later and it turned out to be another dogged victory. Teddy Sheringham and Scholes, who played a brilliant match, scored to beat Newcastle 2–0. Again, the celebrations were muted. It was almost surreal to have won the Double but to be feeling the weight of another big contest to come. After a long, gruelling, emotionally-sapping season, the ultimate challenge awaited.

The Champions League final. At the Nou Camp.

The period between the end of the FA Cup final and the Champions League final seemed to drag. Time slowed down. The sense of history was so heavy, the feeling that this was an opportunity that we might never face again. Nobody was unaffected. Before we stepped out for the final, the manager chose his message carefully, as he always did. 'You don't want to walk past the trophy after the match and not be able to lift it. That would be the worst feeling in the world. To be so close, but to miss the chance to lift the European Cup. Give it everything you've got.'

But, despite those powerful words, we just couldn't get it together in the final. I played in the centre of midfield because Keane and Scholes were suspended. Giggsy was on the right. Blomqvist on the left. Gary Neville, Jaap Stam, Denis Irwin and Ronny Johnsen made up the back four, with Peter Schmeichel in goal. Dwight Yorke and Andy Cole, the partners in crime, were up front.

Bayern scored with a free-kick after five minutes. It seemed to suck something out of us. We just couldn't get it together. As the second half wore on, they pressed home their advantage. They hit the post, then the bar. In some ways, it was almost a miracle we were still in it. Teddy Sheringham and Ole Gunnar Skolskaer came on for Blomqvist and Cole. Time was running out, but somehow we were still alive. The dream was not over yet.

And then the corner. The sign for three added minutes had already gone up. The entire United team came streaming forward, including the goalkeeper. This was our last chance. The Nou Camp is a huge stadium, but there is very little room to take a run-up for a corner. I had to compose myself for a moment and take stock of how to deliver the ball into precisely the right area. I noticed that the United faithful were still roaring. They had seen enough miraculous comebacks that season to believe that another one was possible right here.

I took the corner, delivering it just as I intended into the six-yard box. It bobbled around, was half-cleared, found its way to Giggsy, whose miss-hit shot came to Teddy. In a flash, he turned and hit it first time into the net. I almost did a double-take. The ball had gone in! The game was back on, the Treble was alive, extra time beckoned. But even as I was trying to take it all in, I could see the manager frantically beckoning us back to our own half.

He thought we could win this in the dying seconds. He wanted us to close this out in normal time.

How did he know? Was it optimism, or had he seen the opposition sag? One thing is for sure: Ferguson wanted us to press forward. This was the trophy he wanted above all others, the one he had craved since taking the job. He knew the history: the tragedy of Munich, the Babes, the rebuilding of the club, the first European Cup in 1968. He knew that this was a chance to create history, to put another unforgettable memory in the hearts and minds of fans. We knew it, too. But our legs had gone. The entire team was exhausted. It was only adrenaline keeping us going.

Munich restarted the game, but after a few moments the ball was hoofed up to Ole to the left flank. He tried to take on his man and get a cross in, and it deflected off the defender for yet another corner, on the same side as the last one. This time the roar was even louder. There was a sense of expectation around the stadium, and a sense of dread from the Munich fans and players, that you could almost feel. After 90 minutes when we had hardly carved a single chance, here was an opportunity to score twice in a couple of short minutes and seize the Cup from under their noses.

I ran forward to the corner-flag and caught the ball as it was thrown back to me from the crowd. I struck it sweetly, curving it onto the edge of the six-yard box, as their defenders watched. In retrospect, it was probably the best corner I ever took. Teddy came to meet it, turned it towards goal, and Ole toed it into the roof of the net. Everything went crazy. The stadium erupted. My emotions were raging so fast I almost fell to the ground.

Two goals in extra time. Two goals to win the European Cup. Two goals to complete the Treble.

The entire United squad ran from the bench to greet us as we swarmed around Ole. We were totally overwhelmed: emotionally, physically, spiritually. We just couldn't quite take it in. We were hugging, dancing, grabbing each other. It was only after a few moments that we realised that we had to go back to our own half for the few seconds remaining of the final. We had to repel one more attack, one more potential moment of drama. My legs were so heavy, I would happily have just collapsed.

Thankfully, we hoofed the ball clear after the restart. The Germans' last chance had gone. When the whistle finally blew, I experienced a surge of adrenaline, just enough to propel me towards our fans. Other players were lying on the ground, exhausted. Had it really happened? Had a season full of miraculous comebacks been sealed with the most astonishing climax of them all? Football would never be the same again for any of us. We had achieved something that we would never forget.

After the match, I hugged my mum and dad. My dad could hardly speak for the emotion of it all. I think he was in tears, but then I was, too. He was a United fan, cared deeply about the club before I was even born. And now his son had been involved in perhaps the most memorable night, after the most memorable season, in the club's history.

Victoria was up in the stands at the Nou Camp, as well. She is not a huge football person, but she summed it up perfectly.

'That was incredible,' she said. 'I have never seen anything like it, anywhere, in my whole life.'

Not many players get to hold this trophy. The end of the greatest season of my football career.

History made.

112   *If there is one trophy that needs to be kissed,*
           it's this one.

Pure emotion, sheer joy.

116   *My happiest moment in a United shirt.*

In the Nou Camp looking at the European Cup,
not realising what we had just achieved.

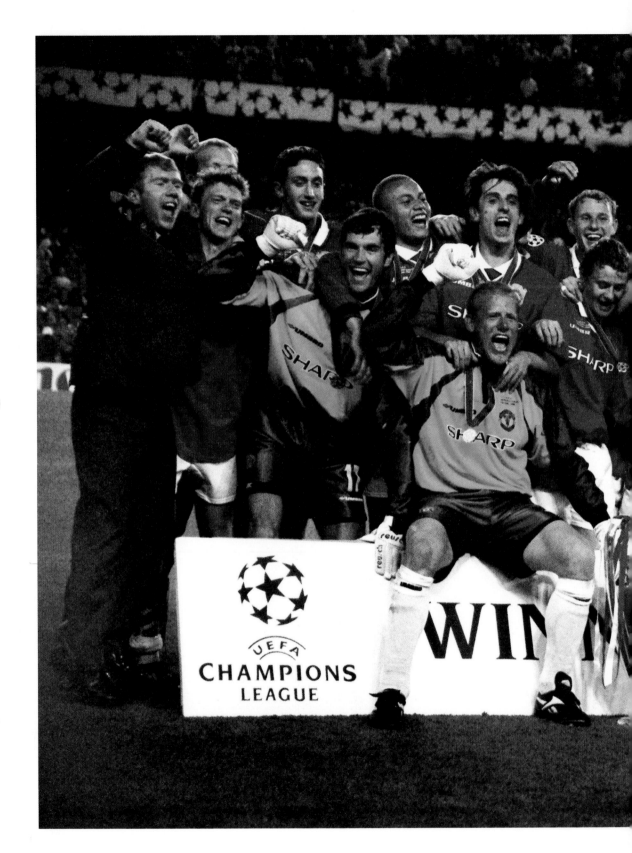

What a season, what a night. One picture to keep.

122   *Loved scoring at Old Trafford.*

124   *Two cockneys.*

126   *My little boy – not so little now.*

130   *Swapping shirts with my hero and the best*
       footballer I've ever played with and against...
       When he asked me for my shirt I was
       in shock.

132   *What a great night with 'Mr United'.*

134   *Best captain I've ever played with.*
        Inspirational and so determined.

136   *Without knowing it, this was the last time*
       I would lift this trophy in a United shirt.

ENGLAND 139

PART TWO

140

No fans travel like our fans.
Thank you for the support
over the years. It's been
emotional and inspiring.

IT IS NOT OFTEN YOU

143

get a chance to exact the perfect revenge. That normally happens in movies, not in real life. In fact, I never really expected to get one back on Diego Simeone and Argentina after what happened in 1998.

But when the chance came, I grabbed it with both hands.

The World Cup is more than a sports competition. It unites the whole country. You see stickers on people's cars, flags hanging out of bedroom windows; football starts to dominate the news. When you take a step back, it is amazing to think that a game with 22 guys kicking a ball around is quite so huge. But then maybe football is more than just a game.

The World Cup meant even more to me as team captain. I knew it meant additional pressure leading the team, but it was also the biggest honour of my life. It gave me a warm feeling just thinking about it. I have always had great pride in my country and a strong sense of patriotism. My country matters greatly to me.

As the tournament approached, and the months became weeks, I felt the excitement growing. The season was still in full flow, but every now and again I would allow my mind to flick forward to July in Japan and the thought of leading out my team, listening to the national anthem, with millions watching on the television back home. I got goosebumps just thinking about it.

Then, just eight weeks before our opening match against Sweden, disaster struck. We were playing Deportivo La Coruña in the second leg of the Champions League semi-finals. A week earlier, in the first leg, I had been caught on the foot with a pretty dangerous tackle. I finished the match (earlier I had scored one of my favourite goals for United, dipping it over the keeper), but the pain was severe, and I left the stadium on crutches.

By the time of the second leg, everything seemed OK. I was moving fine, playing well and I managed to put the injury out of my mind. Then, after about twenty minutes, everything changed. Aldo Duscher, the Argentinean midfielder (why is it always Argentineans?) came flying in for a challenge. His tackle was late, two-footed, with studs showing. It was reckless. He missed the ball completely as I nicked it away, and caught my left foot – precisely on the spot that I had injured one week earlier.

The pain was excruciating, I almost wanted to throw up. I was lying there, trying to get up, but my foot had gone all limp. I couldn't stand on it. The physios had to carry me over to the touch-line, but I was still adamant that I wanted to finish the game. Most footballers hate leaving midway through a match, whatever the pain. The adrenaline tends to numb most of it,

anyway. I told the doctor to give it a good dose of magic spray and to push me back out there. I was certain that I was carrying on.

But then I tried to stand up. It was useless. The pain was so intense, so overwhelming, that I couldn't even put my foot on the ground. It was like nails being driven through my skin. No amount of adrenaline could shut this out. I knew instantly that something was seriously wrong and the doctor confirmed it even as I was lying there. When he took my boot off to feel with his finger around the sensitive area, it was as if my bone was floating around under the surface. I could feel it moving.

'It's broken isn't it?' I said.

'Yes, I think it is.' Came the reply.

My stomach lurched. The pain was one thing, but in many ways it was even more agonising to think about the World Cup. If my foot was broken with just eight weeks to go, I was pretty much finished. The entire dream looked like it could go up in smoke before I had even kicked a ball. How was this possible? Why now? I hadn't been taken out of a match because of injury for a very long time. The timing could not have been worse.

I spotted Victoria and Brooklyn as I was stretchered off the ground and they came with me in the ambulance. That was the only upside as I lay in a state of despair. Brooklyn's face lit up when they turned the blue light on. It was as if Christmas had come early. I couldn't help smiling. I suppose your kids always give you a sense of perspective in a crisis.

And yet I was still desperate to find out the seriousness of the injury. How long would I be out? Was there anything I could do to speed up my recovery? Was there any prospect at all of playing in the World Cup?

The journey from the stadium to the hospital in the ambulance took five minutes flat. Once I arrived, the X-ray was taken almost instantly. You couldn't fault the efficiency of it all. The doctor said that my chance of playing would hinge on what the X-ray revealed. It only took a few minutes, but it was the most nerve-wracking wait of my career.

When the results came through, Victoria went out to hear the news. When she came back, I looked into her eyes, and held my breath. I was trying to figure out if her expression indicated that things were good or bad, but she wasn't giving anything away.

Finally, she told me. 'The bad news is that it is broken,' she said. 'The good news is that you should still be able to play in the World Cup.'

I felt a huge rush inside. I was in with a chance. The dream was still alive.

Over the next few weeks, a bone called the second metatarsal seemed to receive more publicity than almost any other story in the country. The coverage was unbelievable. Almost every national paper was dominated by my foot. Football writers were speculating whether I would be fit enough to lead the team out eight weeks later. Doctors were offering their opinions on the healing process. Faith healers were conducting mass prayers. Very quickly, it became a soap opera.

To me, it seemed like an incredibly short time for a fractured bone to heal. Would my foot really be ready? But the doctors were adamant that, with the right treatment, I would be fit for the match against Sweden on 8th June. All I wanted to do was to work hard to do everything in my power to speed my rehabilitation.

My foot was put in an air-cast, a kind of inflatable boot, by the United physios. It gave me a chance to let the air out and work on the areas around my injury without harming the fractured bone. I could then inflate it before hobbling off. I ran in the deep end of the pool without the foot touching the bottom. I worked out on my upper body and cardiovascular fitness. I worked on my legs. It was gruelling and, at times, monotonous, but I didn't resent a single moment. In some ways, being able to throw myself into the rehabilitation took my mind off the injury.

Before leaving for Japan, the entire England squad flew out to Dubai for a pre-season camp. The families came with us, and it was lovely to spend time with Victoria and Brooklyn before facing up to the moment of truth. The injury was still touch and go. I was working as hard as I could, doing everything the doctors and physios threw at me, but I still wasn't sure if it would be enough. The foot was sore and I could sense that the medical people were still in two minds about whether it would heal.

As the opening game loomed, we had to make a final decision. By now, we had arrived at our base in Japan and it was clear that, if I was going to play in the opening match, I would have to join in full training by the Wednesday. Sven had delayed asking the question for as long as humanly possible, but just after breakfast, he came over, and looked me in the eye. 'Well,' he said. 'Are you fit?'

'Yes,' I said. 'I'm fit'.

I was nervous in my first full training session for eight weeks. My foot was still a little painful and it took me a while to adjust. No matter how much fitness training you do, there is no substitute for a proper game of football, even if it is just in training. I got clattered by Martin Keown early on. That was probably to be expected. He just came in and took me out. Thankfully, the tackle was nowhere near my left foot.

By the end, I was getting up to speed. My foot was a little sensitive; I could feel it, but no more than that. I was on edge all the way to the end of the session, worrying that things might get worse, trying to put the soreness out of my mind, clinging to the hope that I would be able to play. But by the time the session finished, I was totally confident. I was ready.

Leading out my country for the match against Sweden in Saitama will always be one of the proudest moments of my life. When you have the England shirt on, the three lions, and you know how much it means to millions of your countrymen watching in the stands and on the television back home, it is special. It is more than special. These are the moments you live for, the moments you work for. If you are not excited about playing for your country at the World Cup, there is something wrong.

My mum and dad were there, watching. They were always there, watching. I knew how proud they would be, seeing their boy leading out the national team for our first match at the World Cup. It made me well up inside just thinking about it.

We started pretty well. Sol Campbell scored a header from one of my corners near the end of the first half. It should have given us an opportunity to settle and play in the way we knew we could. But, as the second half progressed,

we seemed to lose our balance and composure. Sweden deserved to equalise and, after a rushed clearance from Danny Mills, they got their chance. 1–1.

I was substituted for Kieron Dyer a few minutes later and watched the rest of the match from the dugout. I was angry about the substitution because I felt I had more to give. I guess everyone feels like that when they are taken off.

Afterwards, the entire team was dejected in the dressing room. It was almost as if we had lost the game. It took Sven to shake some much-needed confidence into us. He reminded us that we had every chance to qualify. He reminded us that we still had two matches left in the group. And he reminded us that the next match was vital.

If we lost, we would almost certainly crash out of the competition. If we won, we would almost certainly qualify.

The next match just happened to be against Argentina.

All the memories from four years earlier came flooding back. All the anguish, all the pain, all the consequences that had haunted me. It was almost as if I had come full circle.

Now, I was England captain and had the England fans on my side. This was a chance for payback. Diego Simeone would be on the pitch, and Gabriel Batistuta, who had nodded so approvingly when I had been sent off in Saint-Étienne. In fact, half of both teams were the same as they had been four years earlier.

The only question was: could we reverse the result?

The media went into overdrive. Every newspaper story, every TV interview, every question at press conferences was about what had happened in 1998 and the chance for revenge. England versus Argentina is always a big match. The rivalry has an intense history. We are both major footballing nations with a lot to prove. But this was on a totally different level. It was all about revenge, redemption, destiny. It threatened to overshadow the fact that this was a game of football.

Simeone was a very good player. He had strength, power and was good on the ball. But, he was also a huge irritant. He was always kicking at you, nibbling away at your ankles, trying to niggle you. I suspect that he had targeted me in France in 1998, hoping that he would be able to get an inexperienced player to react to his provocation. In a sense, he had been proved right. Doubtless, he would look for another chance. They all would.

But it wouldn't happen again. That much I was sure of. I knew myself now; I had a much better handle on my own emotions. I knew the kind of things that opposition players might do to provoke a sending off. I wasn't going to fall for it again. Above all, this was a chance to turn the page. A chance for sweet revenge.

The night before the match I phoned Victoria. She could tell I was on edge. She was encouraging, as always. But just before the end of our chat, she relieved the tension. 'Don't do anything stupid, will you?' I laughed out loud. 'I am going to kick someone for old time's sake,' I said.

When the match finally started, the intensity was beyond belief. In the opening few minutes Batistuta lunged at Ashley Cole. He should have been sent off: had it been later in the game, he probably would have been. It showed how much everybody wanted it. Both teams had early chances, but we were having the best of it. Michael Owen hit the post for England.

The atmosphere in the Sapporo Dome was electric. It was like a thumping, surging sensation throughout the ground. This was football from my dreams: high stakes, high passions, high tempo. And we were confident. All the doubts that had surfaced after the game against Sweden had been replaced by a steely determination. Once my foot settled down – it was still sore – I found my rhythm, too.

It wasn't until 42 minutes into the game that the decisive moment arrived. I was on the edge of the area when I was fouled, but the referee, Pierluigi Collina, either didn't see it, or played the advantage. The ball bounced around a bit, before finding its way to Michael Owen, inside the area on the left side. He dribbled past Mauricio Pochettino, the defender, but the Argentinean raised his leg just as Owen went by. Michael went down.

Instantly, I looked at Collina. The Argentineans looked at Collina. The whole stadium looked at Collina.

His verdict was instant. Penalty. England had a penalty.

I walked over to the ball. I could see that Michael hadn't recovered sufficiently from the tackle to take the spot kick. Every single emotion in my body was telling me that I didn't just want this; I *yearned* for it. I needed it. The adrenaline was pumping so fast, I could hardly breathe. I knew that millions were watching back home, and that a new kind of nightmare might begin if I missed, but I also knew that I couldn't turn down this chance to create the perfect ending.

Greece had provided redemption. This was an opportunity to write a final paragraph in the story that I never thought I would have a chance to write.

I placed the ball on the spot and looked up. But as I did so, I couldn't quite believe my eyes. Simeone was standing between me and the goal. I almost smiled at the sight of the man whose career had become intertwined with my own, obstructing a penalty that had just been given by the match referee. I knew what he was doing. It was as blatant as it was cunning. The stakes were already high, but he was raising them just a little higher.

On the face of things, he was talking to the Argentinean keeper. In reality, he was slowing things down, making me wait, playing games with my mind. It was only ten seconds or so, but it seemed to take an age. Just at the moment the referee started making his way towards him to get him out of the way, Simeone started walking – but not towards the edge of the area to take his place. Instead, he was walking directly at me.

It all seemed to be happening in slow motion. What on earth was he doing, I wondered? Was he going to hurl an insult at me? Was he going to threaten me? Was he going to have a little tug of my hair, like last time? All of this was swirling through my mind as the ball sat on the penalty spot, just waiting to be struck.

I started backing away from the ball, but Simeone kept coming towards me. As he got within five yards, I suddenly sensed, to my left, Nicky Butt coming towards us. Then, from my right, Paul Scholes started moving in. They knew exactly what Simeone was up to. They knew that he was trying to get inside my head, to plant a

seed of anxiety before this crucial moment. And they weren't having any of it.

It was a massive moment of reassurance. The pressure was intense but I knew that I had my team-mates with me. My friends. The guys I had grown up with and who had my back. All those feelings of togetherness, that sense of the unbreakable spirit at United, seem to come back to me. I was already feeling good about the penalty, but now I oozed confidence. I had no doubts as I stepped forward.

Simeone's antics had vanished from my mind.

There was another slight delay before I began my run-up. I looked at Collina for the signal to take the kick, then fixed my eyes on the ball. I took a few deep breaths. Finally, Collina blew the whistle and I instantly ran in. I hit the ball as hard as I could towards the middle of the net.

It may not have been the most elegant penalty ever taken, but I instantly knew it was in, and I continued my euphoric run, beyond the area, towards the side of the pitch. I felt a torrent of emotions rushing through my body and mind. I had done it. I had scored against Argentina in the World Cup.

It was not just about revenge, although that was a massive part of it. It was also about the pride of scoring while wearing the armband after so many weeks wondering if I would make it into the starting line-up. Most of all, it was the joy of hugging my team-mates and watching the English supporters going crazy.

Mine turned out to be the only goal in the match. We were ecstatic at the end, celebrating with our supporters on the pitch. We had slumped off without thanking our fans at the end of the Sweden match, which was a terrible oversight. We were not going to let that happen again. We wanted to show our appreciation and to share in the sense of triumph.

Afterwards, we had dinner with our families. When I saw my mum, she burst into tears. My dad was pretty close to crying, too. I knew exactly what emotions they were experiencing; I knew that in their minds, they were reflecting upon what had happened when we had met in the car park in Saint-Étienne. I was high as a kite.

We ended up reaching the quarter-finals in the 2002 World Cup, after a draw in the final group game against Nigeria and then a 3–0 win against Denmark in the first knock-out stage. We lost to Brazil in 100-degree heat that sapped our legs. A fluky free-kick from Ronaldinho didn't help, either. It was from 40 yards out, and he intended it to cross, but his shanked effort somehow dipped over David Seaman and into the goal.

At the final whistle, we were bitterly disappointed to be out of the competition. We had a strong squad, a terrific spirit and, in my honest opinion, if we had clung on to our lead against Brazil until half-time, we could have gone all the way to the final. But it wasn't to be. A quarter-final exit was not what we wanted, and yet it was a decent performance to get there.

But, for me, the 2002 World Cup will always be about that defining moment against Argentina. It was a penalty, but it was also the perfect ending to an incredible, and very personal, story.

Relief.

The goal that would provide redemption.

158 *Nerves like never before.*
Four years of pain and moments
of unhappiness erased in one kick.

160   *Saluting the best travelling fans in football.*

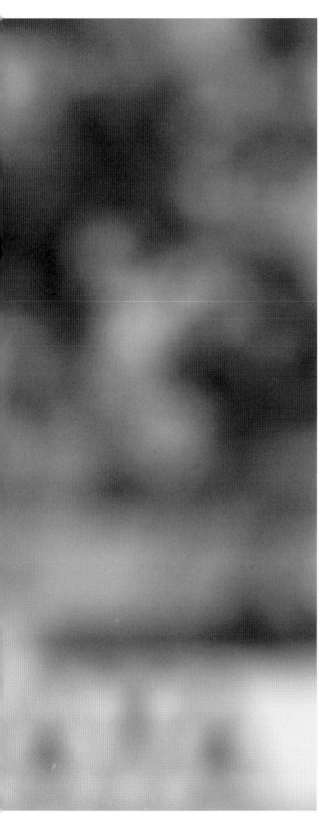

This was a special moment.
Three goals in three World Cups.

170   *Lucky I played well and*
                  scored with that hair…

174 *Management?*
NO WAY.

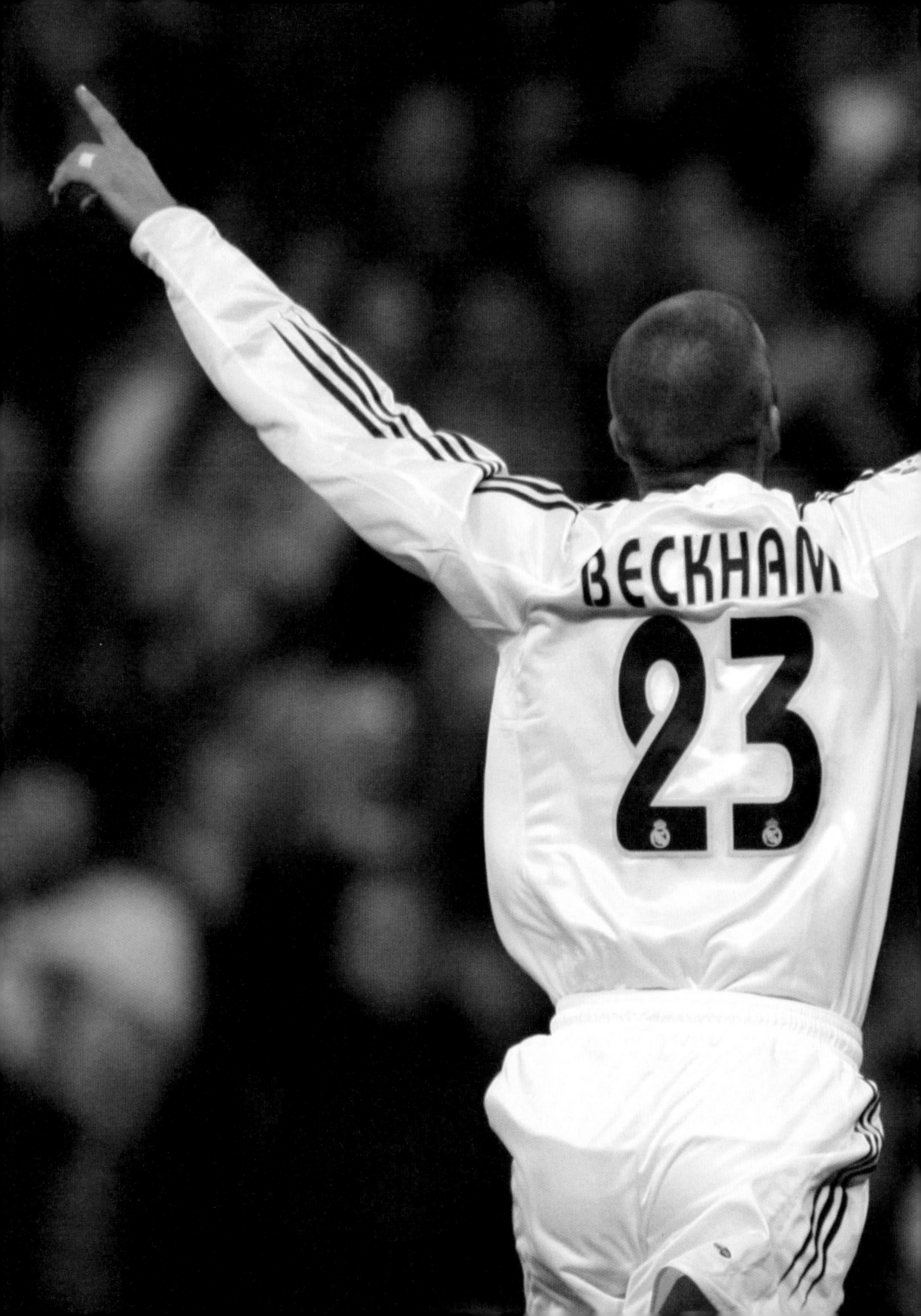
BECKHAM
23

MADRID

I experienced many emotions on this day. Joining a club as big as Madrid and playing with team-mates of this stature was daunting.

ARRIVING AT REAL

Madrid in the summer of 2003 was both fantastically exciting and daunting. For the last 15 years I had been surrounded by people I knew really well. Team-mates I had grown up with from youth team, to reserve team, to first team. The staff at Manchester United were like members of the family. Now, I was walking into a changing room full of players and staff I hardly knew at all.

What would they think of me? How would they react? What if I didn't fit in?

But my deepest concern was how these huge stars would react to the new boy in their midst.

I arrived for my first day early. I got to the dressing room before anyone else and just sat there wondering what to expect. I hoped to make a good impression, but was apprehensive that things might go wrong.

I needn't have worried.

Luis Figo was the first to arrive. 'Hola, how are you?' he said with a bright smile on his face. I was lucky because his English is perfect and he wrote down his mobile number on a bit of paper and handed it over. 'Just let me know if you need any help settling in,' he said. Then Zinedine Zidane walked in; then Raul; then Roberto Carlos; then the rest of the team.

It was amazing to look around at such an incredible group of players. I was in awe of them because of all that they had achieved; it felt a bit weird to be part of the same team. Raul, the captain, handed me a list of two pages of Spanish phrases that I needed to know to do my job. Stuff like 'man on' and 'pass the ball'. I didn't have a problem with doing a bit of homework.

They were laid back, but they were also professional. All my worries vanished. These were great players, legends in the game, but they were also focussed and inclusive. I forgot the fear and allowed my mind to feel the excitement of playing for a new club. This was going to be one of the most incredible challenges of my career.

It had been difficult to leave United, the team that will always be first in my heart. United was the club I had loved since childhood; my friends were there; the fans had backed me to the hilt every time I most needed them.

But I knew that I had been given a great opportunity. Real is a remarkable club, after all. The iconic white strip, the record number of victories in the European Cup, the legion of wonderful fans: it all adds up to a magical place. The Galacticos policy – signing many of the biggest and most iconic names in world football – also added to the sense of wonder.

Over the months, I became completely at ease with my new team-mates. I was particularly close to the Brazilian players in the team. I also developed a strong friendship with Zidane,

who is a great guy. The crowd at the Bernabéu were unbelievable. They are demanding, but they are also crazy about football and passionate about Real.

The only problem I faced from the fans in my time at the club was in a match against Barcelona. We were 2–0 down and the crowd was getting tetchy. The Real-Barcelona rivalry is as intense as anything in world football and the team from Catalonia were in control. As I ran towards the touchline, an older guy stood up and gave me an earful. I looked at him for a moment before turning back to the game.

It wasn't a terrible thing he shouted, particularly when compared with the abuse I had to put up with from away fans in the 1998–99 season, but for some reason it got into my mind. Over the remaining minutes, we got our act together and fired back into contention. Eventually, against all the odds, and with the fans going crazy, we turned the deficit into a victory. It was one of the most brilliant comebacks in all my time at Real.

Afterwards, I ran over to the fan, whose face I had remembered, smiled at him, and then lifted my shirt over my shoulders and handed it to him. He beamed back and gave me a hug. Somehow it felt amazingly good. We had won the match, but I had also won over a detractor. That is always the best way to get someone to change their opinion of you: to work hard and prove them wrong, rather than just getting irritated and shouting back. It was a powerful moment, too, because many other fans were touched by the embrace.

But, despite the many successes in those early years at Madrid, there was also a problem of instability. When I started, Carlos Queiroz was in charge, who I knew from our time together at United. But then he left to make way for José Antonio Camacho, who was succeeded by Mariano Garcio Remón, who was followed by Vanderlei Luxemburgo, whose departure brought the arrival of Juan López Caro, who made way for Fabio Capello. (Luxemburgo and Capello were my favourite two.)

All these changes happened in three short seasons. It was dizzying when compared to United, where Sir Alex was a constant, dominant, reassuring presence. The turbulence did not do much for our title challenge, either. In the first two seasons there were changes of tactical emphasis and training methods and much else besides. We finished second in La Liga behind Barcelona for two seasons in a row. It was difficult for any of us to settle down.

At this time, club President Ramón Calderón was messing about with my new contract and I was missing games. So I had decided to sign for the LA Galaxy on a five-year contract at the end of the season: I was so excited about realising an ambition to help grow football in a country where it isn't the number one sport. But I was still desperate to play for Madrid in my remaining time; still desperate to win La Liga; still desperate to cap my tenure at the Bernabéu with a big trophy.

So I trained even harder. I got to the training ground earlier, left later and demonstrated greater commitment. I went to every match and cheered my team-mates as loudly as possible. I did everything within my power to turn things around.

It would have been easy to have been a prima donna and thrown my toys out of the pram, but

I couldn't allow myself to sit and stew. I wouldn't permit myself to brood on it.

I wanted the club to know that I still believed in myself; that I could add to the team; that I had energy and optimism. I wanted them to know that I wasn't going to just sleep-walk out of the club before my move to America. Most of all, I wanted that La Liga title. I knew how much it would mean to get one over on Barcelona and cap my time with Real with a huge landmark.

The last few months at Real turned out to be the most exciting of my time in Spain. The team started to struggle mid-season and the Spanish players actually went to Capello and urged him to put me back in the starting line-up. That was a huge vote of confidence in me and it made a big impression on the manager. (Later, he would select me to play for my country.) On 10th February, he named me in the team against Real Sociedad. I was on cloud nine. This was the chance I desperately wanted and I was determined to make it pay.

I played well throughout the match, but it was in the second half that the key moment arrived. We were awarded a free-kick way on the right-hand side, from 30 yards out. It was a tough chance, but I knew I had to go for it. I struck it low, just clearing the wall, and it fired into the bottom right-hand corner of the goal.

It reignited my Real career.

It was the beginning of a nerve-wracking run-in as the season drew to a close. In the event, we had to beat RCD Mallorca in our final match to win the title. Although I limped off with an injury towards the end of the first half, we won the match 3–1 with the fans going delirious. I felt a surge of emotion, that wonderful sense that my Spanish journey had ended in triumph.

The club even tried to untie my transfer to the Galaxy at the end of the season. Having been in the shadows, I was a wanted man again. It felt incredible.

It was also special to hear what some of my team-mates had to say. They were some of the best players in the world: by the end, we were almost like brothers. 'We knew about David's qualities with the dead ball and his ability to cross well,' Zidane said. 'But it is impossible to appreciate how hard he works for the team and how much of an unwillingness to lose he transmits until you play with him.'

To hear a comment like that almost meant as much as winning the league itself.

Celebrating with 'Zizou', the best footballer I've ever played with and my friend.

After playing badly in the first leg, I did a lot better at home and even scored with my head.

188   *Russell Crowe eat your heart out!*

My nan and grandad always wanted to visit Buckingham Palace.

>
> NEWTON
> EINSTEIN
> BECKHAM
>
> Own the laws of physics and you own the game.
>
> adidas.com/football

FOREVER SPORT

adidas

194   *Getting off to a great start at Madrid*
       and celebrating with Ronnie. He was
       the best goal-scorer I've ever seen.

Not a bad
five-a-side team…

202 *Wherever I was, I always
looked for the St George's flag.*

It was always my dream for the boys to live my career with me. A great way to leave Spain.

LOS ANGELES

Best way to quieten the away fans.

MANY FOOTBALL 209

experts called America the final frontier. It was said that the richest and most powerful country on the planet would never embrace the beautiful game. Americans had their own ideas, their own obsessions, their own culture.

Over there, it was all about American football, baseball and basketball. They love ice hockey, too. Britain and the USA speak the same language, but when it comes to sport, we are worlds apart.

I signed for the LA Galaxy during my last season at Madrid. Though I had been offered a new contract in Spain, I was ready for a new challenge, a new opportunity. When I spoke to the Galaxy, I liked what I heard.

Simon Fuller had introduced me to the idea that I could have a relationship with the game in America that went beyond my playing days. That I could help grow the sport over there and maybe even one day have my own MLS club. It was an incredible dream.

I knew that moving to America would be a big step. I was only 31 at the time and fully believed that I could still improve my game and make a contribution to the England team. But this was a challenge on an altogether different level. The league in the States was only 12 years old. Football was not tiny, but it was not big, either. I would be joining a league to play football, but I would also be attempting to take the sport into the mainstream. I would be a player but I would also be an ambassador.

It was a chance to make my mark not just on a new club, but on a new country.

When Tim Leiweke, the President and CEO of Anschutz Entertainment Group, came to meet me at my house in Madrid, I liked him at once. He was enthusiastic and honest. I trusted him, and he is a close friend now. 'We really want you to do this,' he said, and I knew he meant it. I found myself warming to the idea. I spoke to Victoria and, after a short conversation, we just looked at each other and nodded. 'Let's go for it,' I said.

It was one of the best decisions we ever made. Our family life was the happiest it has ever been. We were stable, we were together, and it was just fantastic. The sun kept shining and the skies were a beautiful shade of blue. The kids would come home from school and go for a swim, or they would go to the beach. It wasn't long before they started to learn how to surf. The lifestyle was perfect for us, and for the children.

I put everything into my training and matches. I knew there were lovely beaches and tons of opportunities to have fun, but I didn't want to do anything to compromise my preparation for games. My focus never wavered. If I was going to change the way people thought about American soccer, I had to be professional in everything I did on the pitch, and off it. I had to set an example.

Perhaps the biggest problem of all in a football sense in those first two seasons was the same one that dogged my time at Real Madrid: a lack of stability. The manager changed three times and I couldn't help thinking, once again, about the strength that is given to a club and the confidence that is given to players when a manager is given time to make his mark. The success of Manchester United and the long tenure of Sir Alex Ferguson is not a coincidence. He was a great manager, but he also gave the club certainty and reassurance. We knew what to expect, and we knew what he expected of us.

Bruce Arena's arrival as manager towards the end of my second season was a great leap forward. He stayed in the post for the rest of my time at the Galaxy, which was a massive bonus. The team began to perform better and we started to fire on all cylinders. My goal of winning the Major League Soccer Cup was getting ever closer.

The last few seasons at the club were an exceptional time in almost every respect. Family life was still great, and now the football could match it.

I had two loan spells at AC Milan, which were also incredible. In the first I played alongside players like Kaká, Ronaldinho, Pirlo as well as stalwarts of the club like Maldini, Seedorf and Ambrosini. At the beginning people did the usual thing of describing the decision to sign me as a marketing ploy, but after I played a few matches, the pundits had changed their minds. I scored my first Serie A goal in my third match, against Bologna. That was special.

The second loan spell in Milan gave me the most surreal moment in my entire career: playing against United at Old Trafford. I came on in the 64th minute in the second leg of the Champions League and was assaulted by so many emotions it made me dizzy. I had played in the first leg, which was weird enough, competing against guys I had played alongside for years, actually trying to defeat the club I had grown up supporting. But playing against United at Old Trafford, in front of the fans who had supported me for so long, felt like an out-of-body experience.

I was thrilled when the United faithful applauded me onto the pitch. The fans have always been generous like that when a player returns to the club. I could feel the hairs on my neck standing up as I took it all in. We ended up losing the match 4–0 and the tie 7–2, but it felt so special to be back at the stadium that I will always think of as my footballing home, playing in front of supporters who will always remain the most important of my life. Perhaps the experience gave me a bit of closure from the disappointment of leaving United, too. I had never wanted to leave.

This second loan spell with Milan ended badly, however. In the very next game against Chievo Verona, I tore my Achilles tendon. It meant that I had no chance of playing in the World Cup finals for England in 2010 and it took me out of the MLS for the next five months.

The rehabilitation was tough – rehabilitation always is – but I made my return for the Galaxy in September 2010. We ended the season winning the Western Conference title, but we lost to Dallas in the play-offs. My ambition of winning the MLS Cup was still to be realised.

The last two seasons at the Galaxy turned out to be the most successful of all. We were playing to full crowds everywhere we went. People called us the 'New York Yankees of Major League Soccer', because of the extra publicity and interest we generated. It gave me the desire to spend more time on my ambassadorial role, advising the league on new players and how to grow the game. When the name of Thierry Henry came up for the New York Red Bulls, I strongly advised them to buy him. Players like that are vital to the future success of the MLS.

Did I achieve my goal of taking football to a new audience? In many ways, I exceeded my goal. Football was never going to replace basketball or American football overnight, but it did grow to a level that few believed possible a few years earlier. The clubs became more professional and introduced an academy system for the young players. Viewing figures on television and attendances at stadiums took off. The public had a much greater understanding of the game and its tactics. Football was in the mainstream at last.

And, yes, we also managed to win the MLS trophy. Having waited so long, we nailed it in back-to-back seasons. The first victory in December 2011 was special, but when we triumphed for a second time in 2012, it felt like the perfect way to end my American adventure. I had finished my time at Madrid with a trophy, and now I had done the same with the Galaxy. That final match, winning the cup against the Houston Dynamo, was emotional. I draped myself in a Union Flag as I went to lift the trophy, and listened with a sense of incredible pride as the crowd roared.

I knew I had played my last match for the LA Galaxy, but I also knew that I wanted to sustain my relationship with soccer and the United States, possibly as an owner of an MLS franchise. As I said in my post-match interview: I may not play here anymore but I remain just as committed to growing this club, this league and this sport.

In one way, my American Dream had ended, but in another, it was only just beginning.

218   *Another example of my boys*
       living my career with me.

220   *Who better to share a lap of honour with?*

One of my dreams was to go to
the White House as a champion.
It was a huge honour, and to meet
the President was truly an amazing
moment. He questioned my facial
hair: can't blame him really.

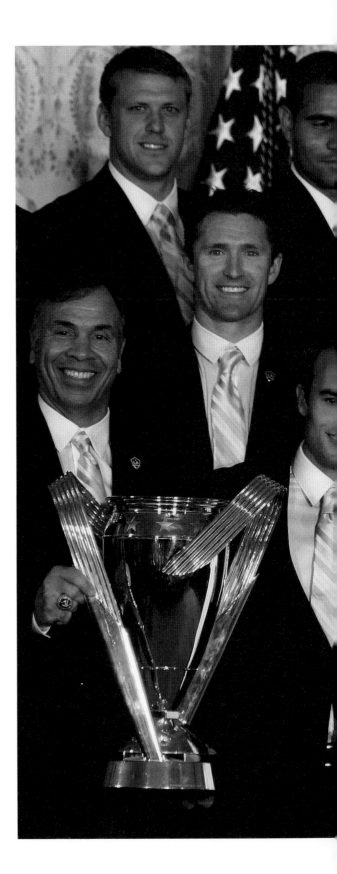

230   *My two girls. So beautiful.*

232   *One more time for LA –*
           with my boys again.

MILAN

235

(Previous page)
Tough challenge but five
minutes after this tackle
I ruptured my Achilles.
Difficult day.

238 *Playing with Maldini, Seedorf,*
Nesta, Inzaghi, Gattuso, to name
a few, and for a club like Milan…
one of the happiest times for
me as a footballer.

Another great player I was honoured to call my team-mate.

242   *First goal for Milan.*

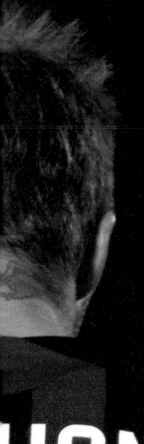

(Previous page)
Quicker than Wazza,
who would have thought?!

250   *Mates together again.*

PARIS

Being so warmly welcomed to Paris 255
by the people and players was one
of the most amazing feelings I've
experienced as a footballer.

I thought I would be able to hold back my emotions on this day but at 67 minutes I started to lose my composure.

IS THIS REALLY THE

257

end? My brain can't quite come to terms with it. Carlo Ancelotti has made me captain for our last home match of the season and we both know that this will be the last time that I will play in a competitive match. The journey that started with kicking a ball in a small garden in East London is about to end in a stadium in the French capital.

I had joined Paris Saint-Germain in January and had hugely enjoyed my time in France. My team-mates were fantastic and it felt really good to donate my salary to a local children's charity. I had always wanted to go out on top, and by winning the French league with PSG, I had achieved just that. It feels right to be retiring, but it also feels awful.

I can't believe my life as a footballer is about to end.

I always knew my final match would be emotional. The game has always meant so much to me: it is more than a passion, more like an obsession. From Ridgeway, my first youth team, to United, the club that will always be first in my heart, and to the matches for England, which made me burst with pride every time I pulled the shirt over my head, football has been at the centre of my life. The centre of my being.

I play the game because I love it: love the competition, love the friendships, love the feeling when I get a chance to strike a corner or free-kick. I have enjoyed being at the clubs that I played for after leaving United: Real Madrid, LA Galaxy, Milan, PSG. Football has taken me around the world and given me a purpose. Playing the game is a part of my identity. It is in my soul and always will be.

But now, as I drive myself forward for one last game, I feel the emotions raging within. They take me by surprise. My legs are becoming giddy as the curtain begins to fall. There will be no comebacks. There will be no second thoughts. This is it. And it is hurting to leave the stage, like a pain that has burrowed into my stomach, like a love affair finally coming to an end.

In the first half, I made one last assist: a corner from the left that was seized upon by Blaise Matuidi, my team-mate. He met it with a left-foot volley that made it over the keeper and into the back of the net. I was desperate to make a mark on the match, to show that I had given it my all until my last moment of competitive action. I am thrilled to have done just that.

But as the second half ticks away, and I know that Carlo is about to substitute me, I am beginning to lose it. My focus is vanishing.

As the bench gets ready to make the change, my chest is tightening. As the substitution is signalled, I can't breathe. I don't want to be emotional, I don't want to cry, I don't want to overshadow the match, which still has 25 minutes to go, but I can't control it. My mind is trying to focus, but it is leaping all over the place. To East

Lifting another trophy in a new country. What a proud moment. It was my last ever game in football.

London, to The Cliff, to Old Trafford, to Saint-Étienne, to Wembley, to Sapporo, to the local field where I whacked those free-kicks against the wire mesh over the window of the community hut.

The tears are streaming as I leave the pitch. I hug my team-mates, I salute the crowd, I look at Victoria and the kids and my family, who I love so much. They are applauding and I know how proud they are. As I leave the pitch, crossing the white line for the last time, I embrace Carlo. And then I sit down.

What next? What will replace football in my life? There will be other challenges, other goals, other exciting things to look forward to. I have no doubt of that. I will always be centred by my family, who mean everything. But nothing will fully replace football. How could anything replace football? The game is like nothing else and anyone who hopes that they will be able to recreate the feelings and emotions of the game after they have retired is kidding himself.

It has been the most incredible, fascinating and emotional journey. I have learned a lot, not least about myself. The challenges have not always been easy; sometimes, they have been almost overwhelming. But I learned to dig deep and to trust in myself. These were important lessons that I will always be grateful for. They made me who I am.

Now, as I look forward to the next chapter, I am content, even as I am filled with sadness. Content with what I have achieved, content with what I have learned, content that I gave it everything. I left nothing out there on the pitch. But then, I guess, that is one thing that will always be true. It is almost a personal motto, something that I try to pass on to my own kids.

Whatever you do in life, give it everything you've got, with a smile on your face.

260   *Emotional day for everyone.*

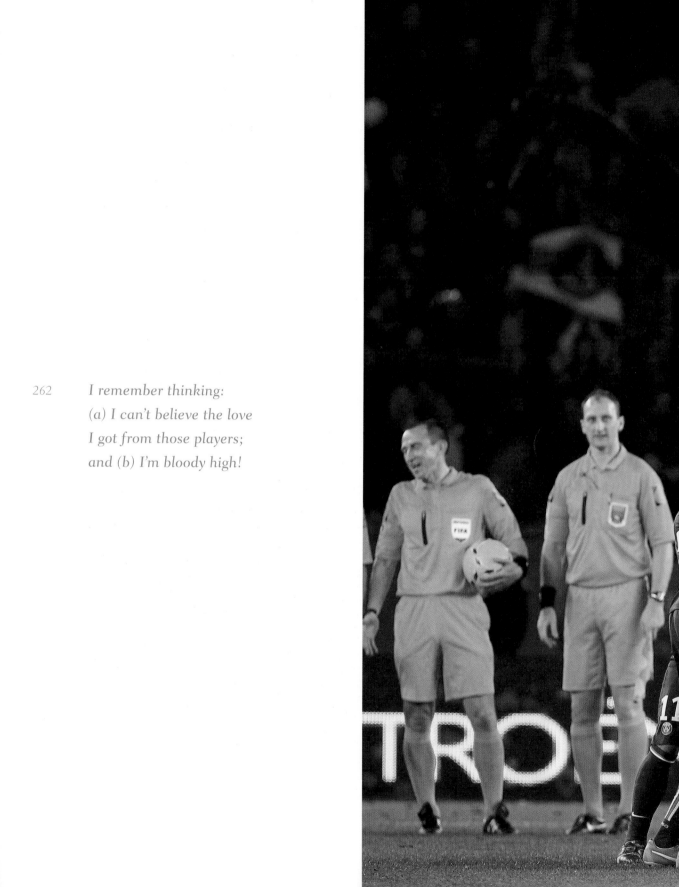

262   *I remember thinking:*
       (a) I can't believe the love
       I got from those players;
       and (b) I'm bloody high!

264   *One last time with my boys as a champion.*
        Thank you for sharing these special moments
        in my life and career. I wouldn't want it any
        other way. I love you boys.

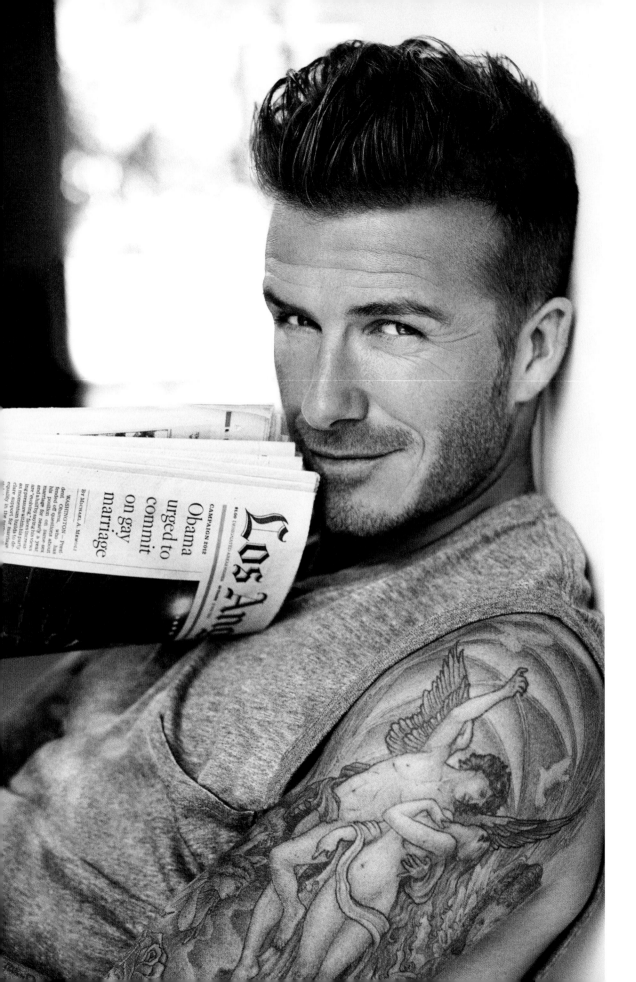

271

272

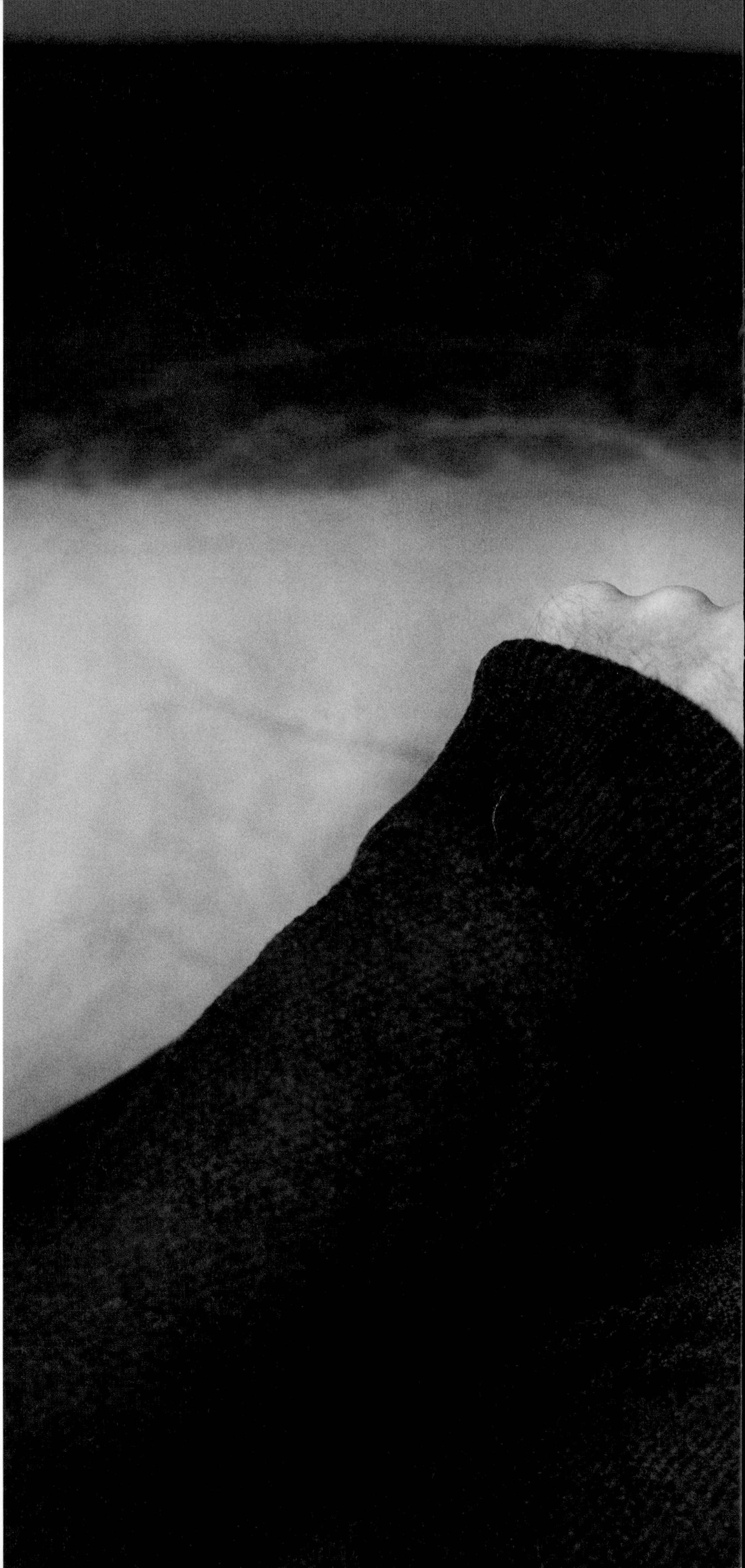

You can see the way boots have evolved over the years.

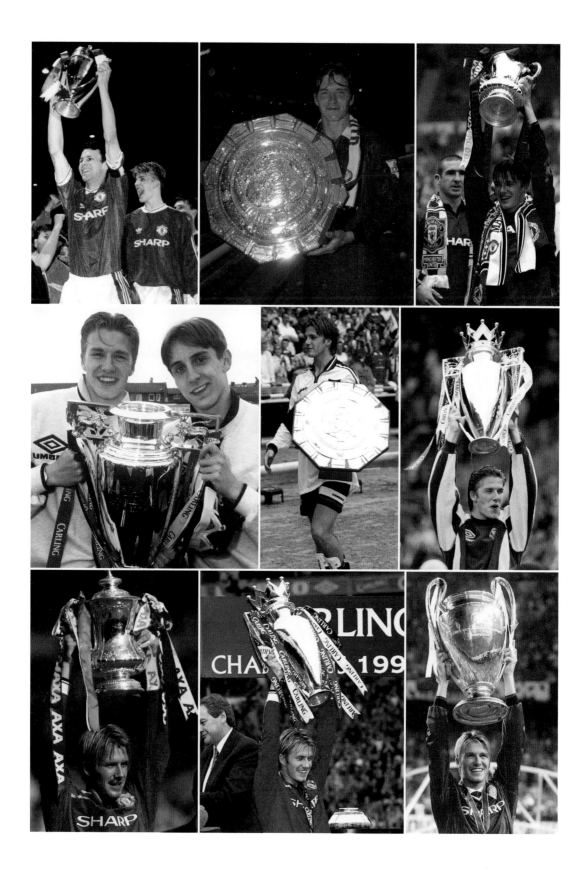

The Fans Faces Project:
over 10,000 of your
photos feature in this
image. Thank you
to every one of you,
and to all of you who
have supported me
throughout my career.

final, Camp Nou, Barcelona, Spain, 26 May 1999. © *Andrew Cowie, Colorsport*

122/123 Manchester United v Chelsea, Premier League, Old Trafford, Manchester, England, 23 September 2000. © *Paul Roberts, Colorsport*

125 Manchester United v Tottenham Hotspur, Premier League, Old Trafford, Manchester, England, 6 May 2000. © *Stuart MacFarlane, Colorsport*

127 Manchester United v Derby County, Premier League, Old Trafford, Manchester, England, 5 May 2001. © *Matthew Impey, Colorsport*

129 Manchester United v Chelsea, Premier League, Stamford Bridge, London, England, 23 August 2002. © *Robin Hume, Rex Features*

131 Manchester United v Real Madrid, UEFA Champions League quarter-final, second leg, Old Trafford, Manchester, England, 23 April 2003. © *Colorsport*

133 Manchester United v Juventus, Gary Neville Testimonial, Old Trafford, Manchester, England, 24 May 2011. © *Nigel Roddis, Reuters, picture supplied by Action Images*

134/135 Manchester United v Everton, Premier League, Goodison Park, Liverpool, England, 11 May 2003. © *Ian Hodgson, NMB Reuters, picture supplied by Action Images*

137 Manchester United v Everton, Premier League, Goodison Park, Liverpool, England, 11 May 2003. © *Martin Rickett, PA Archive, Press Association Images*

ENGLAND (PART TWO)

138 England v Iceland, FA Summer Tournament, City of Manchester Stadium, Manchester, England, 5 June 2004. © *Alex Livesey, Getty Images Sport*

140/141 Italy v England, International Friendly, Stadio Delle Alpi, Turin, 15 November 2000. © *Tony O'Brien, Action Images*

142/143 England v Argentina, World Cup finals group match, Sapporo Dome, Sapporo, Japan, 7 June 2002. © *Matthew Ashton, EMPICS Sport*

150/151 England v Argentina, World Cup finals group match, Sapporo Dome, Sapporo, Japan, 7 June 2002. © *Horacio Villalobos, Corbis*

152/153 England v Argentina, World Cup finals group match, Sapporo Dome, Sapporo, Japan, 7 June 2002. © *Marc Aspland, The Times, News Syndication*

154/155 England v Argentina, World Cup finals group match, Sapporo Dome, Sapporo, Japan, 7 June 2002. © *Andy Hooper, Daily Mail, Rex Features*

156/157 England v Argentina, World Cup finals group match, Sapporo Dome, Sapporo, Japan, 7 June 2002. © *Matthew Ashton, EMPICS Sport*

158/159 England v Argentina, World Cup finals group match, Sapporo Dome, Sapporo, Japan, 7 June 2002. © *Matthew Ashton, EMPICS Sport*

161 England v Argentina, World Cup finals group match, Sapporo Dome, Sapporo, Japan, 7 June 2002. © *Dan Chung PA, JP Reuters, picture supplied by Action Images*

162/163 England v Croatia, International Friendly, Portman Road, Ipswich, England, 20 August 2003. © *Matthew Impey, Colorsport*

164/165 England v Ecuador, World Cup finals second round, Gottlieb-Daimler Stadium, Stuttgart, Germany, 25 June 2006. © *Anders Wiklund, Scanpix, Action Images*

167 England v Portugal, World Cup finals quarter-final, Veltins Arena, Gelsenkirchen, Germany, 1 July 2006 © *Patrik Stollarz, AFP, Getty Images*

169 England v Portugal, World Cup finals quarter-final, Veltins Arena, Gelsenkirchen, Germany, 1 July 2006. © *Kai Pfaffenbach, Reuters, picture supplied by Action Images*

170/171 England v Mexico, International Friendly, Pride Park Stadium, Derby, England, 25 May 2001. © *Andrew Cowie, Colorsport*

173 France v England, International Friendly, Stade de France, Paris, France, 26 March 2008. © *Shaun Botterill, Getty Images Sport*

175 England v Germany, World Cup finals second round, Free State Stadium, Bloemfontein, South Africa, 27 June 2010. © *Jamie Squire - FIFA via Getty Images*

177 England v Slovenia, World Cup finals group C, Port Elizabeth Stadium, Nelson Mandela Bay, South Africa, 23 June 2010. © *Joe Toth, Back Page Images/BPI*

MADRID

178/179 Real Madrid v Levante, Primera Liga, Santiago Bernebu Stadium, Madrid, Spain, 28 November 2004. © *Victor Fraile VF, WS Reuters, picture supplied by Action Images*

180/181 Signing for Real Madrid, Madrid, Spain, 2 July 2003. © *Matthew Ashton, EMPICS Sport*

184/185 Real Madrid v Celta Vigo, Primera Liga, Santiago Bernabéu Stadium, 29 February 2004. © *Rex Features*

186/187 Real Madrid v Real Mallorca, Spanish Super Cup second leg, Santiago Bernabéu Stadium, Madrid,

Spain, 27 August 2003. © *Sergio Perez, Reuters, Corbis*

189 Making of the 'Pepsi Foot Battle' commercial, Madrid, Spain, 4 July 2003. © *Pepsi via Getty Images, photo by Clive Brunskill*

190/191 Receiving an OBE, Buckingham Palace, London, England, 27 November 2003. © *ROTA/Getty Images*

192/193 adidas campaign, 2003. *adidas, the 3-Bars logo and the 3-Stripes trade mark are registered trade marks of the adidas group, used with permission*

195 Real Madrid v Barcelona, Primera Liga, Santiago Bernabéu Stadium, Madrid, Spain, 10 April 2005. © *MarcaMedia, Offside*

196/197 Real Madrid v Real Mallorca, Primera Liga, Santiago Bernabéu Stadium, Madrid, Spain, 17 June 2007. © *Adam Davy, EMPICS Sport*

198/199 Real Madrid v AS Roma, UEFA Champions League Group B, Olympic Stadium, Rome, Italy, 8 December 2004. © *Dylan Martinez, Reuters, picture supplied by Action Images*

200/201 Real Madrid v Deportivo La Coruna, Primera Liga, Santiago Bernabéu Stadium, Madrid, Spain, 26 May 2007. © *Victor Fraile/Corbis*

203 Real Madrid v RCD Mallorca, Primera Liga, Santiago Bernabéu Stadium, Madrid, Spain, 17 June 2007. © *Adam Davy, EMPICS Sport*

204/205 Real Madrid v RCD Mallorca, Primera Liga, Santiago Bernabéu Stadium, Madrid, Spain, 17 June 2007. © *Victor Fraile, Corbis*

LOS ANGELES

206/207 Los Angeles Galaxy v Melbourne Victory, friendly match, Etihad Stadium, Melbourne, Australia, 6 December 2011. © *Brandon Malone, Reuters, picture supplied by Action Images*

208/209 Los Angeles Galaxy v New York Red Bulls, MLS, Red Bull Arena, East Rutherford, New Jersey, USA, 18 August 2007. © *Gary Hershorn, Reuters, picture supplied by Action Images*

212/213 Los Angeles Galaxy v Chivas USA, MLS Cup Western Conference semi-final, Home Depot Center, Carson, California, USA, 1 November 2009. © *Danny Moloshok, Reuters, picture supplied by Action Images*

214/215 Los Angeles Galaxy v Newcastle Jets, friendly match, EnergyAustralia Stadium, Newcastle, Australia, 27 November 2010. © *Brendon Thorne, Getty Images Sport*

216/217 Los Angeles Galaxy v Houston Dynamo, MLS Cup final, Home Depot Center, Carson, California, USA, 1 December 2012. © *Lucy Nicholson,*

Reuters, picture supplied by Action Images

219 Los Angeles Galaxy v Houston Dynamo, MLS Cup final, Home Depot Center, Carson, California, USA, 1 December 2012. © *Stephen Dunn, Getty Images Sport*

221 Los Angeles Galaxy v Chivas USA, MLS, Home Depot Center, Carson, California, USA, 16 October 2011. © *Graham Whitby Boot, Sportsphoto/ Allstar*

222/223 Los Angeles Galaxy v Houston Dynamo, MLS Cup Final, Home Depot Center, Carson, California, USA, 1 December 2012. © *Icon SMI, Colorsport*

224/225 Los Angeles Galaxy v FC Barcelona, friendly match, Rose Bowl, Pasadena, Los Angeles, California, USA, 1 August 2009. © *Graham Whitby Boot, Sportsphoto/Allstar*

226/227 2011 MLS champions Los Angeles Galaxy with US President Barack Obama, White House, Washington DC, USA, 15 May 2012. © *Larry Downing, Reuters, picture supplied by Action Images*

228/229 Los Angeles Galaxy v Houston Dynamo, MLS Cup final, Home Depot Center, Carson, California, USA, 1 December 2012. © *David Bernal, ISI, Corbis*

230/231 Victoria and Harper Beckham, Los Angeles Galaxy v Real Salt Lake, MLS Western Conference Championship, Home Depot Center, Carson, California, USA, 6 November 2011. © *Lionel Hahn/ABACA USA/ EMPICS Entertainment*

232/233 Los Angeles Galaxy v Houston Dynamo, MLS Cup Final, Home Depot Center, Carson, California, USA, 1 December 2012. © *Icon SMI, Colorsport*

M I L A N

234/235 AC Milan v Glasgow Rangers, friendly match, Ibrox Stadium, Glasgow, Scotland, 4 February 2009. © *Jason Cairnduff, Action Images*

236/237 AC Milan v Chievo Verona, San Siro Stadium, Milan, Italy, 14 March 2010. © *Javier Garcia, Back Page Images/BPI*

239 AC Milan v Manchester United, UEFA Champions League, San Siro Stadium, Milan, Italy, 15 February 2010. © *Dan Rowley, Colorsport*

240/241 AC Milan v Siena, San Siro Stadium, Milan, Italy, 17 January 2010. © *Buzzi, Imago, Colorsport*

242/243 AC Milan v Bologna, Serie A, Dall'Ara Stadium, Bologna, Italy, 25 January 2009. © *Tony Gentile, Reuters, picture supplied by Action Images*

244/245 AC Milan v Werder Bremen, UEFA Cup, Weserstadion, Bremen, Germany, 18 February 2009. © *Christian Charisius, Reuters, picture supplied by Action Images*

246/247 AC Milan v Hungary All-Stars, exhibition match, Puskas Stadium, Budapest, Hungary, 22 April 2009. © *Karoly Arvai, Reuters, picture supplied by Action Images*

248/249 AC Milan v Manchester United, Champions League second round, Old Trafford, Manchester, England, 10 March 2010. © *Alessandro Bianchi, Reuters, picture supplied by Action Images*

251 AC Milan v Manchester United, Champions League second round, Old Trafford, Manchester, England, 10 March 2010. © *Mark Robinson, The Sun, News Syndication*

P A R I S

252/253 Paris SG v Brest, Ligue 1, Parc des Princes, Paris, France, 18 May 2013. © *Gonzalo Fuentes, Reuters, picture supplied by Action Images*

254/255 Paris SG v Olympique Lyon, Ligue 1, Gerland Stadium, Lyon, France, 12 May 2013. © *Robert Pratta, Reuters, picture supplied by Action Images*

256/257 Paris SG v Brest, Ligue 1, Parc des Princes, Paris, France, 18 May 2013. © *Gonzalo Fuentes, Reuters, Corbis*

259 Paris SG v Brest, Ligue 1, Parc des Princes, Paris, France, 18 May 2013. © *Gonzalo Fuentes, Reuters, Corbis*

261 Victoria and Romeo Beckham, Paris SG v Brest, Ligue 1, Parc des Princes, Paris, France, 18 May 2013. © *Wenn. com*

262/263 Paris SG v Brest, Ligue 1, Parc des Princes, Paris, France, 18 May 2013. © *Christian Gavelle, Getty Images*

264/265 Paris SG v Brest, Ligue 1, Parc des Princes, 18 May 2013. © *Imago, Colorsport*

266/267 © *Alasdair McLellan for H&M*

269 © *Alasdair McLellan for H&M*

270/271 © *Doug Inglish, Trunk Archive*

272/273 © *Doug Inglish, Trunk Archive*

274/275 © *Paul Wetherell, Trunk Archive*

276/277 © *Josh Olins, Trunk Archive*

279 © *Josh Olins, Trunk Archive*

280/281 *courtesy of Colorsport, Corbis, Getty Images, Sportsphoto and Topfoto*

282 top left: FA Youth Cup, Manchester United v Crystal Palace, 15 May 1992 (© *Christian Cooksey, Mirrorpix*); top centre: Charity Shield, Manchester United v Newcastle United, 11 August 1996 (© *Darren Walsh, Action Images*);

top right: FA Cup, Manchester United v Liverpool, 11 May 1996 (© *Action Images*); centre left: Premier League Championship, May 1996 (© *John Peters, Manchester United via Getty Images*); centre: Charity Shield, Chelsea v Manchester United, 3 August 1997 (© *UPP, Topfoto*); centre right: Premier League Championship, Manchester United v West Ham United, 11 May 1997 (© *Bradley Ormesher, Mirrorpix*); bottom left: FA Cup, Manchester United v Newcastle United, 22 May 1999 (© *HP Reuters, picture supplied by Action Images*); bottom centre: Premier League Championship, Manchester United v Tottenham Hotspur, 16 May 1999 (© *Action Plus Sports Images/ Topfoto*); bottom right: Champions League, Manchester United v Bayern Munich, 26 May 1999 (© *Phil Noble/ PA Archive, Press Association Images*)

283 top left: Intercontinental Cup, Manchester United v Palmeiras, 30 November 1999 (© *Popperfoto/Getty Images*); top centre: Premier League Championship, Manchester United v Tottenham Hotspur, 6 May 2000 (© *Action Images*); top right: Premier League Championship, Manchester United v Derby County, 5 May 2001 (© *IH/BR, Reuters, picture supplied by Action Images*); centre left: Premier League Championship, Everton v Manchester United, 11 May 2003 (© *Martin Rickett/PA Archive, Press Association Images*); centre: Spanish Super Cup, Real Madrid v RCD Mallorca, 27 August 2003 (© *Sergio Perez SP/JV, Reuters, picture supplied by Action Images*); Primero Liga Championship, Real Madrid, 18 June 2007 (© *Angel Martinez, Real Madrid via Getty Images*); bottom left: MLS Cup, Los Angeles Galaxy v Houston Dynamo, 20 November 2011 (© *Lucy Nicholson, Reuters, picture supplied by Action Images*); bottom centre: MLS Cup, Los Angeles Galaxy v. Houston Dynamo, 1 December 2012 (© *Danny Moloshok, Reuters, picture supplied by Action Images*); Ligue 1 Championship, Paris SG v Brest, 18 May 2013 (© *Wang Lili/Xinhua Press, Corbis*)

284/285 England v Azerbaijan, World Cup qualifier, St. James' Park, Newcastle, England, 30 March 2006. © *Ross Kinnaird, Getty Images*